The Other 54

A Hiker's Guide to the
Lower 54 Peaks of the
Adirondack 100 Highest

Spencer Morrissey

Dacksdescents Publishing
Lake Placid, New York

ISBN 0-9786554-1-9

Printed in the United States of America by King Printing
Co-editing by Alan and Barbara Via
Layout by Spencer Morrissey and Drew Haas
Back cover photograph by Nancy LaBaff
All other photographs by Spencer Morrissey

Routes are hand drawn by Spencer Morrissey with maps created by the
United States Geological Survey

Photographs;
Cover: Wallface and MacNaughton from Little Algonquin
Back cover: The author on Dial Mountain

Table of Contents

Introduction

As a teenager I had no real interest in the mountains that shadowed me. Sure I climbed the occasional mountain, but it was more of a field trip in high school-I didn't really have a lot of choice. Growing up in the rural hamlet of Long Lake made me want to live closer to the city and the action. I now find myself happy in the heart of the Adirondacks, amazed at how one's tastes change. My hiking boots now come off in Westport, on a cozy county road where I'm moments from a great number of mountains and trails, and I can see Hurricane, Giant, and Rocky Peak Ridge from my back yard.

My hobby of peakbagging and mountain photography started when I was around 20 years old. On a whim I decided to climb Blue Mountain. That's really all it took and I was hooked. Now I find it hard to skip a day before exploring another peak.

It didn't take long before I had all the trails and mountains in the High Peaks Region traveled. I finished the 46 High Peaks, over time, at age 30. You might ask "What took you so long?" simple, too many peaks and not enough time to climb them all. I found myself climbing peaks like Noonmark, Poke-O-Moonshine, Hurricane, and Owl's Head, and then bushwhacking all the remote peaks that rarely get visited. Mountains like Spotted, Ebeneezer, Baldface, and Camels Hump. Truth be told I'd put my 46er list aside and had come close to climbing my 350th different Adirondack peak before I finished the 46. Upon completing the 46 High Peaks I needed another goal. That's when the completion of "The Other 54" really turned my head. The Adirondack 100 Highest Peaks would be a great list to work on.

At about the 80th Hundred Highest peak, I realized that there are no books that specifically cover the 54 High Peaks that are further down the list after Couchsachraga, the lower 46er summit. Sure there are a lot of guidebooks that give descriptions for the trailed mountains. Try and find one with a description of a route in the challenging Sentinel Range and you'll be looking for a long time. So, with the book in mind and a little persuasion from some friends, I give you this guide into the heart of "The Other 54".

This guide was written to help those wishing to venture off the trails and into the world of contour lines. Since 15 of the 54 have trails, I'll provide brief trail descriptions to those mountains along with some connecting trails. There are also a couple descriptions of bushwhack routes up these trailed peaks; those descriptions will be a little more elaborate. The core of this guide, however, is the route descriptions to the other 39 without trails. Scattered throughout will be pictures from my travels throughout these peaks. You'll find topographical maps corresponding with certain peaks and the trails and routes associated with them. A handy peaks list for all the Adirondack 100 Highest with elevations and associated USGS quads is located in the rear of the book. You can use this as a guide or a planning tool.

This book is intended for use as a reference for the remaining 54 High Peaks whether in the woods or your favorite easy chair. Read the introduction carefully. Off-trail hiking should not be undertaken lightly and I've included a number of common sense and safety precautions any backwoods traveler would be smart to heed before heading out.

This guide was written with the most up to date conditions available when published. But keep in mind that Mother Nature has a mind of her own, and conditions can change over night. Trails could become clogged with downed trees, or rerouted to avoid blow down. Off trail routes can vary from season to season and being 20 feet in either direction could change the entire landscape. With no trail to navigate your reliability to use a map and compass or GPS is very important. Maps included in this guide are also for reference only. The outline of the routes and waypoints are provided as guidelines and should only be used with caution. All routes and waypoints were hand traced by me in reference to my GPS route. These routes are close to those used by me and by those who have volunteered information for this book. Given the nature of these routes, slight variations on the map might put the reader

Mount Colden and Avalanche Mountain from Marcy Dam

hundreds of feet off course. My advice is to use these maps as a planning tool and design your own route.

So, in short, the trails and route conditions are in constant change. The use of this book and the information contained is at the sole risk of the user. Besides, isn't that what exploring is all about?

Dedication and All Around Thanks

 I am dedicating this book to my wife Madeline whose patience in my endless time on the computer, and countless hours in the mountains-has gotten me to this point.

I'd also like to dedicate thanks to my good friend Brian who has been with me on most all of my bushwhacks. Finally, tribute must be paid to my dog Sunny "The Wonder Dog", who's done all of the peaks listed in this guide; maybe the best bushwhacker of them all.

I would also like to send a word of thanks to Alan Via, who not only has hiked beside me on many of these peaks, but has given his time to help with an initial edit of this book. His consistent pressure for me to start writing and willingness to provide me with accurate and vital information to get started will never be overlooked. Of course, I can't forget to thank his wife, Barbara, for letting him. Also, many thanks to those who have joined me in the painful pursuit of the Adirondack 100 Highest by wading through the cripplebush, stepping over blow down, and crawling over slippery rocks through the last few years, and to those who have so willingly helped me gather information to aid me in building this guide accurately.

Thank You,
Spencer Morrissey

Forward

I bumped into Spencer Morrissey by accident a few years ago. As it turned out, we're both members of a very active internet hiking board, Views from the Top. There's a section on VFTT for trip reports and I'd often see really interesting bushwhacks described by a person whose board name was "Peak_bgr". I'd often follow these up with e-mails, asking him about routes and conditions. With the Adirondack 46 and a number of other hiking "lists" under my belt, I thought it would be fun to start another quest, and complete the Adirondack 100 Highest. These mountains are the 54 peaks beyond the first Adirondack 46ers. That 39 of the remaining 54 are untrailed provided the additional allure of difficulty and exclusivity. We estimate that there are fewer than 50 completers, and perhaps many less than that.

"Peak_bgr" would always return my messages, and I eventually learned his real name. With another friend of mine, we arranged to meet for a hike to one of the trailless 54. This was a peak on private land where I had previously secured permission to hike.

It was an early spring day, and I introduced myself to Spencer Morrissey and his constant hiking companion, Brian Yourdon, or "Bushwacker", spring snowflakes floated down. As we exchanged pleasantries, I'm sure they were as curious about me as I was about them.

During the course of this first joint hike, I learned a lot, about them and their obsession with bushwhacking. Over the years, I considered myself a pretty good off-trail hiker. I'd been using a map and compass for 30 years, and with a small group of hiking friends, we always considered ourselves as very competent route finders. This first outing was an eye-opener for me. With Brian handling the GPS work, Spencer jumped into the lead, sniffing out a route up the mountain. Watching him scan left and right, Spencer inevitably found the best way up the ridge.

He was flying up the open sections, around the occasional cliff portions, and over those we could all scale. In the midst of pushing through dense spruce, or clambering over blown down trees, Spencer was always looking for the "path of least resistance" as the key to the reaching the summit. Nor had I ever witnessed someone as intuitively competent with a GPS as Brian. Whether crawling under a fallen tree, balancing on a rock, or plowing through the scratchy stuff, Brian's feet barely touched the ground as he negotiated whatever was in front of him, calling out corrections with GPS in hand. I'd never seen anything like it.

Besides what I saw on that first day, I came to realize that Spencer and Brian had more accomplishments than doing these mountains. To give you an idea of Spencer's "credentials" for writing this guide, he's climbed over 600 different Adirondack mountains, bushwhacked around 400 of them. He has a goal of climbing every named peak in the Adirondacks some day. So far, he's climbed every named peak and bumps on 12 Adirondack map quadrangles, with 12 more quads nearing completion.

In the intervening time, since that first hike, we've come to be good friends. We have done many of the 54 together. In addition to learning more bushwhacking than all the experience I'd picked up in the years preceding, I'm grateful to "the boys" for getting me to places I'd have never gone on my own.

I hope you enjoy this guide. A lot of work and effort went into its writing and it can help you to experience some of the great hiking experiences it will open for you.   – Alan Via

Private Land

Some of the routes in this book are over private land-and will be mentioned as such in the trail description. Some routes only cross private property-these will also be pointed out in the trail description for that specific mountain.

When crossing private land it is important to get permission from the landowner, lessee or the caretakers of the property. This is one of the most logistically challenging parts about completing the Adirondack 100 Highest.

Some lands are leased by fish and game clubs. These clubs have certain rules they must follow too keep their leases. Some of these clubs may require payment of a year's membership to their organization; while some may ask for a partial year's membership. This protects the club from liability issues and fulfills their requirements set by the land owners themselves.

Remember: Get permission for passage over these lands. You can do what we did, which is use the contact information often provided at the entrance roads, or go in to meet the members on a weekend when you feel they are probably present. In order to protect their privacy, I am unable to provide any personnel information about the land owners and caretakers.

Types of Routes

Trail- Is a route that is marked with foot trail disks-either placed there by the DEC, ATIS, or other organizations.

Path- Is a route that is similar to a trail but can be intermittent and is lacking foot trail disks, but may be marked with ribbon or paint blazes.

Bushwhack- Is a route that has no trail or path recognizable-traveling through the woods by means of map and compass or GPS.

Avalanche Lake

Winter Travel

 There are only a handful of people who have finished the Adirondack 100 Highest. Many fewer have accomplished this challenge in the depths of winter.

Winter travel on trails can be hard, but for the most part these trails have been broken out and previously packed. But, remember when leaving the trail and venturing into the woods there will seldom be any broken route. Problems can arise when traveling through unbroken ground. For example; snow bombs can fall out trees on those passing underneath, causing you to quickly get wet and cold. Large amounts of snow could accumulate on the branches of spruce trees, but not fill in under the branches. This is called a spruce trap. You can not see these small traps but can walk over them without realizing it. Then the next one you may fall through. This could also get you cold and wet really fast-as well as turning an ankle or god forbid break something. Some spruce traps can get as deep as 10 feet, making it hard to climb out-this could also cause your snowshoes to become trapped under the snow, making it hard to get free.

The nice thing about winter bushwhacking is; it's easy to find your way out of the woods, just follow your tracks out. The only thing that could change this is a storm, heavy winds and/or continuously falling snow.

Slide climbing in winter is another story and involves more care. The terrain is steeper and often icy, so crampons most often are needed. While avalanches are rare in the Adirondacks, they do happen-so always keep that in the back of your mind.

Hypothermia is as easy to get in the Adirondacks as it is to get in any other part of the world. To prevent it be sure to stay dry, well hydrated and fueled, and always be prepared for the unexpected.

Dehydration is as just as easy to get in winter as in the hotter months.

Winter conditions on Morgan Mountain

Bushwhacking in winter can be wet and cold,
Wilmington Range

The problem is you just don't feel it the same way, or as soon. Drink even if you not thirsty. Remember, the cold temperatures and deep breathing from exertion cause you to loose moisture. Very common symptoms of dehydration in the winter is cramping, and lack of energy.

As you can well see winter hiking and climbing can be fun, exciting and a little more risky. Just remember to think ahead, and always be prepared even if the weather looks good, and your chances of a safe day in the woods looks even better.

Duck Hole

Safety Tips for the Backcountry

The first and foremost thing you can do before you leave the house is to let someone know where you're going and an estimated return time. Leave the name of the mountain and the planned route, if something does go wrong, you'll be located much faster.

Cellular phones are seen a lot in the mountains now, but the reception can be very limited, and in some spots non-existent. It's not a bad idea to have one, but don't depend on it as a main source for help. If for some reason you do get lost, stay calm and look around for some familiar landmarks-maybe a brook, a near-by mountain, or the sound of cars. If you're well prepared you should have a map with you, and the landmarks will be on that map. Then if all else fails stay where you are, and that note you left at home will do its job and lead people to you.

One other important thing you can do to help yourself out is-make a checklist. You know things you need to bring on a hike. A few examples are;

- Food/snacks
- Water
- Dry socks
- Flashlight/headlamp
- Camera/film
- Extra batteries for light
- First aid kit
- Matches
- Rain jacket
- Map/compass
- Sunglasses

For winter you might want to add a few things, and get a slightly larger pack. For example;

- A small closed cell foam pad to sit on or for a cold barrier
- Emergency blanket or sleeping bag
- Dry shirt
- Extra base layers
- Snowshoes
- Crampons
- Gaiters
- Toe/hand warmers
- Extra gloves/hat
- Face mask/goggles
- Gore-tex jacket/pants

These are only a few examples of thing I may bring on a day trip. The hike and length of trip may dictate what to bring. Your list should be built to suit your individual needs.

Safety is probably the most important thing you can consider when planning a trip, especially when you leave a trail and start bushwhacking. Remember the chances of meeting or seeing another person off trail is unlikely. Lastly, remember it's never too late to turn around. Consider setting a turnaround time and stick to it. The mountain will be there tomorrow.

If an emergency does arise be sure to have a local Forest Rangers phone number on hand. These can be found in most all trail registers. If you are starting a hike where there are no trail registers be sure to keep an emergency number on hand. Each region will have different contact numbers. The High Peaks Region will use Ray Brook, while the Indian Lake Region will use a local Forest Ranger.

Hiking and Bushwhacking with Kids

Hiking with kids can be fun, but yet can also be a challenge. You need to know the kids abilities, because in their mind they can do anything.

Some of these peaks have trails that lead to the summits, which makes them easier than the trailless peaks-but can still be a tough challenge for a child. In fact if the plan is to start this list with a child, start with a mountain that has a trail, then slowly work your way up to an easier bushwhack. Then once your in the woods you can see how you child does, without diving right in. In fact a child standing around 4 feet tall gets all the branches right in the face, as well as the small shrubs you will pass through. Here are a couple thoughts;

- Make the hike fun, not a race to the top. Let your child be the first to the top, it gives some a feeling of accomplishment. If they do start going to fast, stick a rock or two in their pack that will slow them down-just kidding.

- Let them invite a friend their own age, someone on the same ability level, so they don't feel left behind.

- Let them lead and carry a pack, so they feel like a part of the group and that they're doing their part. Start their pack off a little lighter, and add to it as they get a little older and stronger.

- Encourage them to keep a journal of their trips.

- Buy them a camera of their own so they can take some pictures to share with family and friends. This may help keep their interest longer and take their mind off the long parts of the hike. It also gives them something to look back at, as a good experience.

- Make the hike comfortable. If you wouldn't wear it, don't assume they would. Have them break in new boots, just as we would. Bring those dry socks-kids just love water and mud. If they're comfortable, everyone wins.

- Make sure they snack and drink along the hike-this will keep their energy up and their positive attitudes. I swear to this day, my daughter climbs for the beef jerky and dark chocolate.

- Be sure to let them know how they're doing, be positive. Give them many words of encouragement.

- Don't get into the "we're almost there" routine, it's never ending-and you're almost never "almost there".

- Most importantly, don't tell them there's ice cream at the top unless you're climbing Whiteface.

There are many keys to hiking with children; these were only a few suggestions that I found out to be helpful on the trail. All children are different in their own special way, and only you know what that is. Remember, the fun starts with you.

Having fun on the Blue Mountain fire tower

Rules, Regulations and some Common Sense

When using a lean-to it can be occupied by anyone until it reaches its full capacity. No tents can be set up in a lean-to. No group can be camped in one lean-to for more than three consecutive nights or be larger than 10 people without a permit. When camping, the site should be at least 150 feet away from any water source or trail, unless it is a designated site. Always carry a tent, don't depend on a lean-to being available.

- Some lean-to's have been removed, but are still seen on maps. Check first to see if the site is still there.

- Campfires are a ton of fun and are great to keep warm on those cold nights. However in the Eastern High Peaks Region, campfires are prohibited. Some outlying areas are also off limits to fires. So, all fires should be limited to designated areas, check the regulations in the area before you set off on your trip. Only dead and down wood can be used, cutting of live trees is highly prohibited.

- All human waste should be buried at least 8 inches deep-and 150 feet from any water source or trail.

- All dogs need to be leashed while on hiking trails and at public camping areas, when in the Eastern High Peaks Region. Dogs are not required to be leashed off trail.

- Camping is prohibited above 4000' in elevation. Camping is only permitted in designated areas above 3500' in elevation.

- A bear canister is also a requirement for camping in the Eastern High Peak Region. Campers found not using one are subject to a sizable fine. Its scent proof and a bear cannot penetrate the smooth round surface. Be sure to keep it at least 100 feet from your campsite. The hanging of a bear bag is not an adequate precaution.

- Bears are always a problem and in some areas it may be inevitable that you will encounter a bear or hear one during the night. After cooking be sure to clean up completely. Clean all your dishes and pans thoroughly. All cooking and clean up is recommended to be done away from your tenting area or the lean-to.

- Hiking groups need to be limited to 15 individuals or less.

- When bushwhacking in larger groups, stagger your line. Don't have everyone hike in the same line-this causes a trail to develop and unnecessary erosion.

- Most importantly, leave no traces. If you carry it in, you can carry it out, don't litter. If you see litter, pick it up. Always leave the area as nice, if not nicer than you found it. That way the next person can enjoy it as much as you did.

- Do not cut trees, alter views, or deface any mountain to better your experience. You may like it, but the next person may take offense-and it's just wrong.

- If you are going on private property, remember it's illegal to do so without the land owner or managers permission. Plan your hike and get permission first. If you get caught you could be arrested and fined, and it would be no ones fault but your own. Just consider this another friendly warning.

Contacts and Private Peaks

Below is a list of contacts and the private peaks that are near them. I only included organization names to keep the individuals privacy intact. To get phone numbers and other contact information, the homework is going to have to be done by you the climber.

Salmon Pond Game Club
Southern approach to Fishing Brook Mountain #88, Fishing Brook Peak #91

Minerva Fish and Game Club
Northern approach to Fishing Brook Mountain #88, Fishing Brook Peak #91

East River Club
North River Mountain #57, Cheney Cobble #74

Elk Lake Lodge
Boreas Mountain #65, Sunrise Mountain #77, Wolf Pond Mountain #95

Deer Valley Club
Panther Mountain #54, Buell Mountain #64, Brown Pond Mountain #100

Ragged Mountain Club
Wolf Pond Mountain #95-Southern approach, summit is on Elk Lake Property

High Peaks Stables
Carriage rides into the Santanoni Preserve and Moose Pond Region
Little Santanoni #89-approach and summit is on state property.

Finch and Pryne
Dun Brook Mountain #85-closed to hikers at this time.

Abbreviations

GPS- Global Positioning System

JBL- Johns Brook Lodge

AMR- Adirondack Mountain Reserve

ATIS- Adirondack Trail Improvement Society, associated with AMR

ADK- Adirondacks

FT or '- Feet

Ht- Height

DEC- Department of Environmental Conservation

SOA- Shore Owners Association

HP- Herd path

TR- Trail

BW- Bushwhack

RT- Round trip

Rte- Route

Mt- Mount

Mtn- Mountain

E- East

Abbreviations

W- West

N- North

S- South

SE- Southeast

SW- Southwest

NE- Northeast

NW- Northwest

Studying the map at Wallface Pond

Glossary

Bump- A small summit or peak, usually found on a ridge of a much taller peak, can be of various size and shape.

Cairn- A pile of rocks (usually cone shaped) that marks a route or the summit.

A large rock cairn marking the route on the Jay Mountain Ridge

Col- Is also known as a valley or passes between two peaks.

Corduroy- Logs placed side by side to help form an old woods road or trail through a wet or muddy section.

Cripplebrush- A band of thickly studded growth, usually found at higher elevations.

Death March- A term used when a hiking out from a long days adventure. The hiker is usually very tired and uncomfortable.

Duff- Decaying plants or leaves that form a soft underfoot.

Femur Eater- This is a hiking term for when a hiker falls through an unseen hole. Most holes are covered by a light layer of duff and/or leaves.

Fernwhacking- A play on words. Fern used in replacement to bush. Rather than hiking and pushing your way through trees and bushes, ferns are in its place.

Glissading- A term used when sliding down a steep snowy section, either on your feet or your butt. Using either a hiking pole or ice axe to slow down or help change direction.

Logging Roads- Unmarked and very roughly built roads used to haul logs out from the forest, many of which are now exempt or unused.

Non-Conforming Structure- A structure or piece of equipment placed in a wilderness area, which are not naturally part of the area. Fire towers and canisters are often seen as non-conforming structures.

To some a fire tower is a non-conforming structure, Hurricane Mountain

Slide- An open avalanche track, often steep and exposed.

Looking down the Kilburn Slide

Spruce Trap- When snow develops on the tops of spruce branches leaving air pockets underneath. Waiting for a unexpecting passerby to step on and falls through.

Vly- Also known as marsh or meadow.

#47
MacNaughton Mountain
Elevation 4000'
Map #1

At a resurveyed elevation of four-thousand feet this peak should have made the original list of 46er summits. However it was not recognized by the 46ers when the list was made by Russell Carson. Therefore, it jumps right to the head of the class of "The Other 54". To this day is higher than 4 of the original 46 and someday maybe formally recognized and added to the 46er list. It could happen.

MacNaughton was originally named Henderson, but was changed by Verplank Colvin in the late 1800's. Because of its elevation being 4000' this peaks popularity is rising, and now has many approaches to its summit.

The summit has nice views as well as a few from along the ridge and the middle peak, such views as; Street and Nye, the MacIntyre Range and Henderson Lake below.

*Via Wallface Ponds
*Trail/Bushwhack
*Red Route

The route you will take starts from the Adirondack Loj, and follows the trail toward Rocky Falls and Indian Pass. The trail starts on the opposite side of the road as the Loj parking and heads toward Heart Lake. The trail is gradual with only a couple small climbs up to the junction where the Rocky Falls Trail comes in. After another 2 mile stretch over a rocky and usually muddy trail, are Scott Clearing and the intersection with the Wallface Ponds trail.

The trail from here is about 2.7 miles to Wallface Ponds. The trail climbs almost immediately to the height of land before moderating out. After a quick 1.5 miles you will pass by Scott ponds. Don't mistake these for Wallface Ponds; you still have a little over a mile to go.

Checking out a flume along MacNaughton Brook

The trail from here gets pretty sloppy and wet, crossing streams and old corduroy. The route to the summit starts near the third pond furthest to the W. You will have to make you way around the immediate pond to the south and cross the swampy outlet into the southern pond. This will bring you to the smaller pond at the base of MacNaughton. The total distance to the summit from the far end of the pond is roughly 0.8 miles and under a thousand feet of elevation change. We found the going to be rather open and uneventful for the most part-but people have been running into thicker sections and small areas of blow down over the past few years. The best route we have found is to head straight for the middle peak, and cheating to the south a little if the going gets a little thick.

The views are pretty nice from the middle peak, but the true summit is the NW peak where there are more views to the north. There once was a 46r canister on this peak, but has been recently removed and replaced by a wooden summit sign.

Approx. distance: 7.5 miles
Approx. time: 9 to 10 hours RT

*Via MacNaughton Brook from the West
*Trail/Herd Path
*Black Route
This route is becoming the most popular approach to this 4000 footer. However, the going is somewhat blocked by recent blow down.

On this day we set out to get #99 for our close friend Alan Via. The morning was wet from dew collected on the trees, and dirty from the seemingly never-ending mud pit that led us toward Duck Hole.

It was a modestly early morning at Upper Works/Tahawus where the black flies of early summer hounded our every step; but that didn't damper our moods, we were getting #99 done today.

MacNaughton Mountain

We started along the trail from Upper Works and continued the approximately 5 mile trek to the brook that drains MacNaughton. The trail has some ups and downs, some slippery corduroy, a couple shaky bridges, and some half rotted walk ways. But in just over 2 hours we were standing at the sight of the herd path. Marking the herd path is four pieces of old relics left behind by the loggers, many years ago. The four pieces of metal lay along the trail on the right just few yards from the brook I mentioned above. This point is roughly 0.4 miles past Hunter Pond. We found this to be a great spot for a short sit down. Having a quick snack and making a few friends with the local dragonflies, we got some added energy for the unfamiliar territory we were about to discover. We heard rumors of a herd path along the brook, aided by flagging, but slightly hindered by recent blow down; so we expected the worst, but hoped for the best. Well, we got a little of both.

The herd path is quite apparent behind the littered metal, which soon reaches the shore of the brook and a rarely flagged herd path (as of October 2006). It doesn't waste much time climbing above the brook, and a rather tall flume. The flume can't be seen from the herd path, you will need to go to the brook to see it. We continued along the herd path, which meanders in and out of the brook, but mostly followed closely to the shore. In spots we found ourselves pushing through some thick overgrown areas, climbing over sizable boulders, and doing an obstacle course over fallen trees. But that's all in a day's fun. The herd path is well planned, returning to points of interest along the brook, like tall waterfalls, cascades, and flumes.

Then the challenge started. We came to a lone flag, and now had to do some work. Meaning? Not just that there was no path to follow, but a blow down field of thickness and despair demolished the path. We tried to find it and only accomplished getting scratched and frustrated. We bailed out into the brook and rock hopped what we could; only returning to the woods when rocks were unavailable. Looking to the right of the brook we noticed small sections of a herd path which in turn got us around the blow down and by the sections of brook that had little to no rocks to hop. Once out of the blow down area we noticed a small herd path on the left. We decided to follow this to its end. It's in nice shape, very light, but easy to follow for most of the distance. When it did finally end, we were only minutes from the end of the brook, and rock hoping this section was as easy as rock hoping can be. Soon we were at the end of the brook. It just disappears into the side of the mountain, go figure. But hallelujah, there's a flag. A much older version, faded, cracked, and breaking apart, but it at least gives us some hope of a future summit. We had lost a good half hour if not more fighting that deadfall section.

This old herd path followed a contour that brought us almost directly to the summit (roughly 0.3 miles away), not along the ridge we had expected to approach. The path was very easy to follow with no real blow down to mention. Only slightly did we loose the path, but we stopped and looked and soon found a small ribbon a few trees up. This herd path brought out all 85 degrees of the heat we were experiencing that day. It got rather steep, and we found ourselves having to put one arm through, then the next, then the pack; just to squeeze through the closely-knit trees.

Then the herd path ended on the ridge 0.15 miles from the summit, along another very clear ridge herd path. This path we found going in both directions along the ridge, and with a quick check on the GPS we needed to go left to the summit. Minutes later we sat, black fly infested, on the small summit of MacNaughton. On the summit is a state sign reading as such. Views are only off in one direction. Almost the entire Sawtooth Range is visible, as well as the Sewards. Half hidden to the far right is the many ridges of Lost Pond Peak. After we relaxed and compared war wounds from the climb we decided to retreat to our ascent route. But upon our return to the blow down section we knew exactly what to expect, making it much easier to navigate.

Not a bad day in the woods though. 10 hour round trip, 10,000 scratches, 2 quarts of blood, 7 black and blue marks, 12 femur eaters, half a million various biting flies, 12 miles on the odometer, one really wet foot, and three smiling faces-got to love it.

Approx. distance from Upper Works: 7 miles
Approx. time: 8 to 10 hours RT

*Via Wallface Ponds Outlet
*Trail/Bushwhack
*Blue Route
This 1.5 mile bushwhack to Wallface Ponds southern pond is very
beautiful and relatively easy.

Start from Upper Works and follow the Indian Pass Trail past the
Wallface Lean-to at 2.5 miles. From Upper Works the trail starts out
along a road for 2 miles. The road is very wet in spots and some careful
footing is needed to stay dry on the trip in. You will quickly come to an
intersection where the road splits, stay left. The road now has a slight
climb and descent which delivers you to a second intersection with a
trail to Duck Hole. This time go right as the road is now a trail. A half
mile past this intersection is another trail junction stay left and you will
very soon be at the Wallface Lean-to, an excellent spot to take a break.

The route, which is the outlet from Wallface Ponds, is the second major
stream crossing from the NW past the lean-to. Following along the
brook and at times in the brook you will pass by many small waterfalls
and flumes and open slabs, a great start to a beautiful hike. The route
steadily ascends, and the stream turns into a gorgeous vly. This open
field of green is probably one of the nicest spots I have found in the
Adirondacks. The brook meanders all through the deep grass and shrub
entangled banks of the vly. The footing is very soft, feeling as though
you would fall through. This is a very fragile area; I'd encourage you
to view the vly from afar. The brook from here is more cascades and
waterfalls-just an all out joy of a hike.

Once at the pond, skirt the pond to the west and take a heading just
south of west to the summit ridge. The woods from here are surprisingly
open and once on the ridge a herd path will lead you the remaining
distance.

35

Approx. distance from Upper Works: 5.25 miles
Approx. time: 8 to 9 hours RT

MacNaughton Brook

Along MacNaughton Brook

*Via drainage from the SE
*Trail/Bushwhack
*Green Route

This was the first route I took up MacNaughton, by mistaking it for the drainage of Wallface Pond-a very nice error.

To access this route; take the first brook crossing past Wallface Lean-to; 0.25 miles up the trail. For trail information into Wallface Lean-to; see "Via Wallface Pond Outlet". This brook is more of the same-waterfalls and flumes and rock slabs. In low water and non icy conditions you will be able to hike in the brook along the slabs for a good portion. Just below a mile the brook goes underground and the route climbs very steeply with soft/wet underfoot, and slippery at times. The woods here are very open along the really steep sections, but when the gradient lessons the woods seem to close in a little. This route will emerge you in the most southern peak of MacNaughton this is NOT the summit ridge. There are small views from here but after a short descent and about a 200 foot climb you will be on the ridge and the views will pop up along the apparent herd path.

Approx. round trip from Upper Works: 5 miles
Approx. time: 7 to 8 hours RT

#48
Green Mountain
Elevation 3980'
Map #2

Green Mountain is found almost directly north of Giant Mountain and due to its scarcity of climbers, you probably won't see much information on it. Green is most likely climbed a couple times a year and some of that is by repeat hikers. It's not reclimbed because of the spectacular views but because of its solitude and ease of passage. Below are four routes to the summit, some more hiker-friendly than others.

*Via Slide Brook
*Trail/Bushwhack
*Black Route

This is the least traveled route, but a fairly scenic one. Follow the Giant Mountain Trail that starts from Rte 9N just outside of Elizabethtown. The trail to this route is a very moderate climb over a well broken in path, and begins along a dirt road. Stay on the trail for just over a mile to the Slide Brook crossing. Here, you pick up the bushwhack by following Slide Brook upstream for about a mile. Sometimes you will find yourself in the stream to avoid thicker vegetation along the banks. At just under a mile-0.8 mile to be a little more exact; is a second fork in the brook, follow the left fork upstream which will disappear in a little over 0.6 miles. The latter portion of the brook is littered a little more with blow down, and becomes much steeper ascent. The climb for the next 0.25 miles soon becomes very steep up the peaks shoulder, before it starts to moderate and top off on the summit ridge. The true summit is just beyond to the W. The summit boasts no views but you will discover a few along this route. If done in the winter, you'll see more.

The Other 54

Approx. distance from 9N: 3.5 miles
Approx. time: 6 to 7 hours RT

*Via the East Ridge
*Trail/Bushwhack
*Green Route

The East Ridge was once a wonderful route to the summit, but over the last few years, has become more cluttered with dead fall and a lot of brush has grown up to choke the once easy passage.

The bushwhacking route starts at 2.6 miles along the previously described trail, and at the Owl's Head Lookout junction. Here is the place to turn NW and climb to the first bump along the ridge-at 0.5 miles from the trail. The second bump along the ridge is reached in another 0.5 miles. The going here is still decent even with the moderate blow down-and the views that keep popping up are nice as well. You are now along a flat section of the ridge that lasts quite a while before again climbing the last 1.2 miles and 840 feet in elevation to the top. The ridge gets a little thick in spots and the crown around the summit is the last push you will need to make.

Approx. distance from Rte 9N: 5 miles
Approx. time: 8 to 10 hours RT

*Via the Giant Lean-to
*Trail/Bushwhack
*Blue Route

This route is actually across the trail from the lean-to, and what a nice place to start out if you're camping overnight. This is by far the best route to the summit, and the quickest.

From the Junction with Owl's Head Lookout, continue over the height of land and descend to the valley graced with tall maples. The trail will

40

flatten out with a slight climb to High Bank at just over 4 miles. From here there are great views of Rocky Peak Ridge and Giant. The trail now is moderate to the lean-to intersection where the route to Green begins.

The summit is only 0.6 miles away-straight up. It's 830' up to be more exact. This is not by far the steepest route up an Adirondack peak, but it is a workout. Enter the woods from the trail and begin your climb up a steady hardwood covered grade. The woods are extremely open, and enjoyable. On the way up be sure to look back every now and then to see the Y shaped slide on Giant-very impressive, loads of fun. The only thick part you will encounter is the summit crown, in the last 0.1-0.2 miles.

This route is the shortest, but if you start too much further up the trail, it becomes very thick and overgrown. I learned this first hand when my first bushwhack was from the Giant Mountain Intersection. The time to Green's summit from the Giant Mountain intersection is at least double.

Approx, distance from Rte 9N: 6.25 miles
Approx. time: 7 to 8 hours RT

*Via Putnam Brook from the West
*Trail/Bushwhack
*Red Route

This was once a popular route to this wooded summit. However, with blow down getting worse over recent years, it's becoming a route I wouldn't recommend to anyone. The reason I touch on it here is to update climbers of its conditions I have become aware of. If after reading this you decide to try it, the more power to you.

Start the hike from Rte 73 along the Mossy Cascade Trail to Hopkins. The trail follows the brook at first before following a road for about 0.3 miles then leading into the woods. The trail is very pleasant to walk, with a very nice short side trip to the base of Mossy Cascade Falls. The trail is very steep in places and doesn't really offer any breaks until just before the junction with the Ranney Trail which leads back to Rte 73. From here the trail is very steady to the junction with the East Trail and Giant and the Hopkins Trail. It is a mixed, up and down hike for the next 0.75 mile climb to the Putnam Brook crossing.

Y Slide on Giant from Green Route

Your route to the summit follows the brook at this point. The battle begins almost immediately. What once used to be somewhat open in the beginning is now cluttered with blow down. The going gets very thick, with visibility of only a couple yards in front of you. Your climbing partner could be 15 feet away and unseen. You should plan on about 1.5 hours to go the last 0.75 miles; possibly some of the thickest stuff in the park.

Approx. distance from Rte 73: 4.5 miles
Approx. time: 9 to 10 hours RT

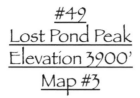

#49
Lost Pond Peak
Elevation 3900'
Map #3

Lost Pond Peak is a name given to this mountain because somewhere up there, there's a pond-but no one knows where. What? You don't believe me? Actually Lost Pond rests just below the summit of this unofficially named peak. In fact, the mountain isn't even specified on any maps, it's just referred to as such. You can find it located north of Lost Pond and south of Street Mountain.

*Via Scott Clearing Lean-to
*Trail/Bushwhack
*Blue route

The first section of this route follows the Indian Pass Trail from the ADK Loj. (See MacNaughton via Wallface Ponds, page 30 for trail details.) After an hour to an hour and a half of hiking you will come upon a lean-to.

From here head directly west and cross Indian Pass Brook-this may take a little navigating to find the best spot, especially during times of high water; once across the brook, climb steeply over the first embankment into the evergreen forest. The climb is steady and in spots a little overgrown-nothing to ruin a nice days outing. It is rocky in spots underfoot, so watch where you step. After climbing steadily and moderate for 0.5 miles, the terrain gets a little steeper, and the duff underfoot gets even more unstable. It isn't a continually steep, but the very short breaks in climb are few and far between.

At 0.8 miles and just before the ridge and first bump there is a very nice view spot. A huge boulder sitting on the shoulder of the ridge is the

43

ticket. Climbing it for the views is a little tricky but can be done with some care on the back side. The view of the ridge and the entire MacIntyre Range is worth the effort.

Once the views have been taken in, climb down off the perch and continue west to the ridge. The first bump is just under a mile from the lean-to. At this point you will want to head 0.2 miles north along the ridge to a second bump and the start of the true summit. You will descend only about 50 feet in elevation to the col between the two bumps and climb a little more. The second bump is the shoulder of Lost Pond Peak at 3820'. The summit is 50 feet higher and to the NW. The mostly flat ridge is very thick and takes some time to push through. I'd recommend avoiding the sub summit by skirting it to the E, coming into the col, and then going for the true northern summit.

The summit has some magnificent views, and in the winter even better when standing on many feet of snow. To the N is Street; to the S is the twinkle of Lost Pond. The views to the E are dominated by the entire MacIntyre Range. This is a very breathtaking viewing area. Even with the partially blocked views, it's referred to as one of the Adirondacks best kept secrets-even though it's not really a secret.

Approx. distance from the Loj: 5 miles
Approx. time: 8 to 9 hours RT

*Via Scott Pond Trail
*Trail/Bushwhack
*Red Route
Refer to "MacNaughton via Wallface Pond" for brief trail description up to Scott Pond.

Start again from the ADK Loj and follow the Indian Pass Trail for 3.7 miles the intersection with the Scott Pond Trail-follow here for another 1.1 miles to the height of land just before the trail descends to the shore of Scott Pond. From here head NW along the ridge through a semi-open forest and on a steady-steep grade. At 0.5 miles from the trail you ascend the first bump along the ridge. You then have a short drop of about 90 feet to a col along the ridge, before a steep climb of 350' to just above Lost Pond itself. I'd suggest that you resist the temptation to descend to the pond unless you want to navigate the difficult trek back to the ridge. The pond is very nice with the ridge totally surrounding it, but there is a cliff in the way of circumnavigating it. The pond is stagnant water, not recommended for drinking, but it's amazing what a good filter can do. This ridge as mentioned is very thick in spots and is dotted with cliffs and drop offs along the way-eye protection would be a very wise idea. There are a few small bumps to climb over on your way to the summit,

Approx. distance from the Loj: 6.25 miles
Approx. time: 9 to 10 hours RT

*Via Outlet from Col
*Trail/Bushwhack
*Green Route

This is becoming a more popular route to the summit, but is less direct. Again follow the Indian Pass Trail from the ADK Loj. This time you will only be on the trail for 2.6 miles before you will take a heading W and cross Indian Pass Brook.

At this point there is a very obvious fork of the brook that acts as drainage for the col between Lost Pond Peak and Street. It is very obvious and hard to overlook. Only 0.15 miles from Indian Pass Brook lay a wonderful waterfall that is worth the trip all by itself. The hike along the brook is quite open, but filled with "femur eaters" as we like to call them. These are soft spots in the ground between rocks or tree roots that are covered up with years of falling leaves. When you step on one, your leg falls in until either your foot hits bottom, or the falls is stopped by your crotch hitting the ground. At around 3000' leave the brook and hike up the slopes to the E summit. The woods to this point are surprisingly open, but the peak will soon extract its price for the easy

45

conditions as you approach the summit.

Approx. distance from the Loj: 5.6 miles
Approx. time: 8 to 9 hours RT

*Via Street Mountain
*Trail/Bushwhack
*Black Route

Start your day from the ADK Loj and follow the Indian Pass Trail for 0.6 miles just past the Trail Register and head right as if heading to Mount Jo. Not far up the trail a sign reads no maintained trail beyond this point-that is the herd path to Street and Nye Mountains. The path is very easy to follow and very soft underfoot. It first drops significantly to the shore of Indian Pass Brook, where you will have to ford or rock hop. From here the trail is moderate for some distance before climbing steeply to an intersection. Right is Nye, left is Street. There is an "S" and an "N" carved on a tree in the intersection. Make sure you go left. The path here is very pleasant, a real joy in my book. There are a few well eroded spots along the way-which makes this more like a route than a trail.

Street has a very nice view from a perch just after the summit; sitting on this rock you will be able to see your route ahead. From here the bushwhack begins. It is very thick for a good distance from Street's summit. The routes than begins to slowly open up before reaching the col between Street and Lost Pond Peak. The descent is around 700 feet over the 0.75 miles-pretty steep and steady. From the col it's a nice walk through fairly open mixed woods forest to the summit crown where it gets thick once again.

Approx. distance from the Loj: 5 miles
Approx. time: 10 to 12 hours RT

Iroquois from Lost Pond Peak Ridge

Lost Pond Peak from shore of Lost Pond

#50
Moose Mountain
Elevation 3899'
Map #5

Moose is found NE of McKenzie Mountain just outside the Village of Lake Placid. On older maps you may have trouble finding this mountain, because it was once named St. Armand. This peak is often combined with McKenzie for a longer 100 Highest double. The Shore Owners Association's (SOA) maintain a series of trails in the area, some of which lead to Moose and McKenzie. Moose is a very enjoyable peak with a lot to offer, from its spectacular views to its lightly traveled trails. Before I can write on any of the SOA Trails I need to send a grateful shout out to Richard Hayes Phillips. He took it upon himself to reopen the SOA Trails along Lake Placid, Moose and McKenzie Mountains. A sole man with the help of a few individuals, located, cleared, rerouted, marked with SOA disks and signed every mile of the trails we use today to enjoy this area. I join the many hikers that thank you for your time and effort in completing and maintaining what some said couldn't be done.

*Via Wadsworth Trail
*Trail
*Green Route
For a trail description to McKenzie Mountain from Rte 86 or the Whiteface Inn, see the McKenzie Mountain chapter (page 72) of this guide.

You will have the choice of making the climb to the summit of McKenzie either from Rte 86 or the Whiteface Inn, both trails have there pros and cons but the reward remains the same.

The Other 54

From the summit of McKenzie continue over the top and descend slightly for about 0.2 miles into a saddle and to the trail junction with Moose. The junction is marked with a nicely hand crafted sign.

From the junction expect to see the trail a little obscured with blowdown. In some cases we had to stop and look for the trail to immerge from the wreckage. Luckily the blowdown didn't last long, and is cleared once a year; as we were told by the gentleman doing the clearing. We shortly found ourselves at a small spur trail that leads to an amazing view toward Whiteface, at 0.2 miles. Upon our return to the trail we found ourselves on a steep descent to the col with McKenzie and Moose. The climb started again almost immediately from the col to a small hill with open woods, and another spur trail to a view of McKenzie Mountain, at just over 1 mile. We then had to descend yet again into another col with this hill, before leveling off for a while. Yet another spur trail? Yes there was, at about 1.5 miles. We later found out this goes down to a small marsh sometimes referred to as Clearwater Spring; a source of Two Brooks.

At 1.5 miles we were at the lowest point along the ridge at 3620'; according to our GPS. This is where we started our climb to Moose Mountain. Along this steady climb of Moose we passed two more spur trails with views off each side of the mountain. We decided to pass on these as clouds were starting to roll in, and the views would be non-existent anyhow. From here it is a steep ascent up the last leg of Moose Mountain. At times it was very narrow with trees lining the sides; it has a very High Peaks feel to it. Then at 2.9 miles we were on the sweet views of Moose; Lake Placid most prominently seen below.

Approx. distance from McKenzie: 2.9 miles
Approx time: 1.5 to 2 hours, one way

Bartlett Pond on the way to Moose Mountain

*Via Bartlett Pond Trail
*Trail
*Blue Route

The Bartlett Pond Trail is located off the SOA Lake Trail approximately 0.9 miles from the Whiteface Inn Road. We started this day early under a bluebird sky. Haze was minimal due to the passing rain the day prior. The Bartlett Pond Trail is only level for just over 0.1 miles, before it begins a gentle ascent. At around 0.25 miles we sat and had a snack on an old stone dam before our climb to Bartlett Pond. This is a most pleasant hike, gentle, soft, and quiet. The brook always within reach, sounded soothing to the ears. Then at around 1.75 miles we crossed the brook near its outlet from Bartlett Pond.

We followed the trail from here as it swings around the NE shore of Bartlett Pond to a pleasant grassy shoreline. A partially submerged canoe rests along its shore. The colors here in the autumn are breathtaking, with each shade reflecting off its placid water. From here the trail makes a sharp turn right and delivered us onto its relentlessly steep grade up the ridgeline of McKenzie. We later checked our elevation gain along this section, and to our surprise, we gained 1100' in just 0.85 miles.

At 2.25 miles we found ourselves at the trail junction to Moose Mountain, which is referred to as the Wadsworth Trail. From here it's just 0.25 miles top the summit of McKenzie. We really enjoyed this section of trail. It's a narrow walkway along an equally narrow ridge. The summit of McKenzie marks the start of a DEC Trail that leads to Rte 86 and the end of the SOA Trail.

For the Wadsworth Trail section of this route see the previous description.

Approx. distance from Whiteface Inn: 5 miles
Approx. time: 5 to 6 hours RT

*Via Two Brooks Trail from Lake Placid
*Trail
*Red Route

This is one of my favorite approaches; the woods are so quiet, uneroded, and full of life. We started off our day again at Whiteface Inn, and used the Lake Trail as an approach to the Two Brooks Trail. The start of the Two Brooks Trail starts 0.5 miles up the Bartlett Pond Trail which is roughly 0.9 miles from the Whiteface Inn Road.

From the intersection on the Bartlett Pond Trail we descended to the brook and carefully crossed it. It can be a very tricky spot to cross, especially during high water, which was our case. Once across the brook we noticed a private trail on the right, which is now closed to the public. Please do not use this trail as an approach to the Two Brook Trail. Following the public trail to the left we found ourselves on a somewhat rocky course before starting a steady climb at 0.4 miles from the brook. Still climbing I found myself fighting an imaginary rock in my shoe, which I never did find. The trail is very moderate, with only a few steep pitches here and there. Then at 1 mile we decided to rest along a small brook to snack on cashews and dark chocolate, before we started a short steep climb.

The trail then turns into a gentle hike for almost 0.6 miles to a side trail junction to Loch Bonnie; that enters on the right at 1.75 miles. This area was totally devastated by a winter storm back in the 90's; the remnants are still obvious today.

We then had to descend into a small col before a steep climb along the remaining trail to Moose. We enjoyed many views back toward Lake Placid and the High Peaks along this steep section. Then at 2 miles we came to some large cliffs along the left side of the trail; cold to the touch, and wet with moss. Just beyond here we came to the ridge and the junction with the Loch Bonnie Trail. The summit is just beyond 100 yards to the left.

The Other 54

Approx. distance from Whiteface Inn: 3.25 miles
Approx. time: 4.5 to 5 hours RT

*Via Loch Bonnie Trail
*Trail
*Black Route

We were pleased to see this trail had been cleared and maintained, especially not knowing what to expect. We found this trail located just up from Camp Solitude across a small bridge. Upon finding it we quickly jumped in, awaiting the newness we would find around every corner. The trail was so soft; it felt like virgin forest under our feet. Loads of ferns and young hemlocks lined the trail with their fall beauty, almost encroaching at times.

We found ourselves with an initial steep climb for the first 0.1 miles before coming to an old woods road, that we would follow for another 0.2 miles; where it then becomes a footpath. At 0.6 miles we came to a major junction with the trail to Undercliff; also an excellent starting point for this route to Loch Bonnie. We were very please to find this trail on a gentle slope. This gave us time to enjoy the open coniferous forest without the struggle of a steep climb. However, we knew this would end, and at 1 mile it did. It became a very steep ascent for 0.2 miles to a point where Minnow Brook crossed the trail. Then it mellowed out again and climbed for 0.25 miles before a gentle descent to Loch Bonnie at 1.4 miles. After a short distance we found ourselves standing in a meadow, enriched by yellow, orange, and red foliage. To our left stood a very old lean-to; it's fully equipped with a dirt floor, leaky roof, a well laid out pine bough rug, and a family of really friendly bull frogs. Who could ask for more?

We found that the trail crosses the meadow over a very wet stretch of tall grass. Care is a must, if dry feet are important. It's was a short distance to the other side and dry land, but we could see this as problem in the spring, or after a few days of heavy rains.

Just outside the meadow there is a trail junction. Left goes over to the Two Brooks Trail and straight up the hill goes to Moose Mountain. We opted to go for the direct route to Moose. From here it is a relentlessly steep climb; one of the steepest I have ever been on. It's almost a 1000' climb in 0.5 miles. We could not believe what we were on. Almost a quart of water along this leg of the trail was in order; a breather about every few hundred feet was also a good choice. But, we loved it. We reached the trail junction with the Two Brooks Trail at around 2 miles from Camp Solitude. From here we only had a couple hundred feet left to the summit.

Be sure to check out the other SOA Trails for many loop possibilities. The Wadsworth Trail, the Two Brooks Trail, and the Bradley Pond Trail all have wonderful qualities and shouldn't be missed.

Approx. distance from Whiteface Inn: 4.2 miles
Approx. Time: 5 to 6 hours RT

Loch Bonnie

#51
Snowy Mountain
Elevation 3899'
Map #4

This mountain is by far the most popular mountain in the area-as you will see by the consistently full parking area. Not only is the reward a 360 degree view from the fire tower, but if one was so inclined to look, views can be had in all directions from the ground floor. Snowy lies just off Rte 30 outside Indian Lake, and lacks being 4000 footer by only a hundred feet. Enjoy the climb it's a beauty.

*Via Buell Mountain
*Bushwhack
*Red and Blue Routes Route
See chapter on Buell Mountain in this guide (page 108).

*Via State Trail off Rte 30
*Trail
*Blue Route
This is the only route with a trail up Snowy, and of course the most popular. This 3.8 mile hike is a challenge, with its total ascent being around 2100'-which is more than some of the High Peaks. The trail winds through old growth forest, and over boardwalks that cross muddy areas. Then after 1.25 miles of relatively flat hiking you reach the first crossing of Beaver Brook, having climbed only 300'. You will cross the brook two more times along the trail before you hike along side it at the 2 mile mark. The trail will now take you through a small draw that the brook follows for about 0.4 miles before exiting westward and steeply

out. The 1.2 miles from here to the summit is where all the work begins with 1450' more to be climbed. The route zigzags, then at just under 3 miles the trail follows open slabs, with roots protruding from the sides, and heavy erosion underfoot. The good news is that excellent views back toward the High Peaks waits a short ways above. With most of the climb over, you can scramble the couple hundred feet up to the site before exiting westward and steeply out. The 1.2 miles from here to the summit is where all the work begins with 1450' more to be climbed. The route zigzags, then at just under 3 miles the trail follows open slabs, with roots protruding from the sides, and heavy erosion underfoot. The good news is that excellent views back toward the High Peaks waits a short ways above. With most of the climb over, you can scramble the couple hundred feet up to the site of the old observer's cabin, and take in some excellent views from various points. A maze of herd paths will lead you to them. Just beyond and a couple feet higher to the west is the fire tower. Be sure to bring your camera here on a nice autumn day, the foliage is breathtaking.

Distance from Rte 30: 3.8 miles
Approx. time: 5 to 6 hours, RT

View from Snowy Lookout

#52
Kilburn Mountain
Elevation 3892'
Map #6

 Kilburn is one of four Adirondack 100 Highest peaks that reside in the Sentinel Range. It also boasts the best views of the four.

*Via North Notch
*Bushwhack
*Blue Route

At one point this wasn't considered a bushwhack but a trail leading to a bushwhack. The trail now is all but gone. The North Notch Trail was once a nordic ski trail for the 1932 Winter Olympics. To find the start of the trail follow Riverside Drive in Lake Placid for three miles-from the Lake Placid side. The road is directly across from the Olympic ski jumps. After just over 3 miles on the right you will see a small brook that goes under the road and into the Ausable River. There is a small parking area right near this spot, along with an old rock monument.

The trail is well trod for the first mile then becomes less and less visible, before it turns impossible to follow. The best way to assure that you get into the notch is to keep the swamp to your left and take a heading east. On some maps it shows the old trail starting on the left of the brook, but this side is just as difficult to follow, and you want to be on the opposite side of the swamp. From the marshy area, the height of land in the notch is 2.4 miles. The climb is almost 1400' over those 2.4 miles-through a nice open forest. There are some patches of blow down and dead fall, but nothing to serious.

From the notch, Kilburn is located to the north 1.3 miles. The ridge willtake you over 3 smaller bumps before topping out on the actual summit-bump #4. The going will be very challenging, thick, even a little painful unless prepared with eye protection and long clothing. The good news is you won't loose a lot of elevation in between the knobs along the ridge. The summit is a little beaten down from the visitors but that may be the only sign of humans you will encounter. The best views are a little beyond the summit to a ledge. Views of almost the entire Sentinel Range are visible, not to mention a good look at the High Peaks.

This next route description is a great descent route as well if a second car is available for a spot.

Approx. distance from Riverside Drive: 4.25 miles
Approx. time: 10 to 11 hours RT

*Via an inlet near Monument Falls
*Trail/Bushwhack
*Red Route

This was my second adventure up Kilburn, and I must admit, it was much more enjoyable than the first. This route we used as a descent route for our first hike to the top, which was a route via the slide. That trail description is also in this chapter. So, rather than taking the chance of losing an eye or quart of blood on the other route, we decided to follow this "easier" route. "Easier" is a relative description in the Sentinel Range.

Proceed to a parking area at Monument Falls, off Rte 86 just outside Lake Placid and near Wilmington Notch. There is a trail directly across the highway that follows an old road that is now extinct. We followed this trail for roughly 0.25 miles to a small stream crossing. We followed this small brook for a short distance until we came to a small flume type gorge in the brook that we needed to get around. We chose to go to the left of the stream to avoid it, not a good idea. It's very thick on that slope. On our descent, we came down the opposite side of the brook. It was much nicer and I'd recommend you go right when you reach the flume on your way up.

Head steeply uphill through nice open woods and gain the top of the ridge. There is a nice sized cliff that can be easily skirted or even climbed along one area. We descended right over the cliff through a narrow dirt area, using trees for balance. The area crossed back and forth along the entire height of the cliff, with only a short jump near the bottom.

Shortly, you'll meet back up with our ascent route. It's a very open area along the lightly flowing brook. You'll come across a small waterfall over open slabs that we climbed to the top, and the woods continued to be bushwhacker friendly. We entered a small open area, almost a field, with large amounts of skunk cabbage-truly and unusual spot in the Sentinels. Looking around, we found remnants of an old hunting or logging camp, including an old whiskey bottle, rusty bucket and other artifacts.

Our route planned to keep us below the ridge and out of the normal thick travel, ridges usually entail. But we found that the valley along the brook had lots of new growth evergreens, and the slopes heading up the ridge looked to have open hardwood coverage. I'd recommend you follow our way upward, taking the steep ascent with a slight side hill angle to the ridge. To our delight, the ridge had an open black spruce canopy. The scattered blow down mixed in was a little bit of a hassle, but not terrible and I'd estimate that 50% of the ridge was nice walking. When the ridge got to thick we dropped 40' to 50' in elevation to the left of the ridge's crest, the woods opened up and made for much quicker and easier travel. By following this tactic the ridge became very bearable. As we neared the top on the last slope, we noticed a herd path developing to the summit-just before the summit is the point where the views begin.

You see Whiteface, Moss Cliff as well as the other Sentinel Peaks. The best spot, though, is just feet down from the summit to the top of a small rock ledge. It's adequate for about 3 people, or in our case, two people and one canine.

Approx. distance from Monument Falls: 2 miles
Approx. time: 6 to 7 hours RT

*Via the Kilburn Slide
*Trail/Bushwhack
*Green Route

The Kilburn Slide is not recommended unless you have some slide
climbing experience. Wet rock or a slip can lead to a serious injury or
worse. The upper portion or "headwall" is very steep, climbing this is
unnecessary, even though inviting.

This route starts across from Monument Falls and follows the trail
described in the above route to where the slide rubble crosses the trail.
The rubble leads to the slide you will be climbing. From the trail, follow
the washout for a couple minutes and the slide will appear to the left.
There is a natural staircase to the left at the base of the slide, start here.
The slide is fairly steep, and the rock is grippy. However it can be very
slippery in the wet areas. The slide doesn't last as long as many, but is
a challenge and very exciting. At its top, the slide has a headwall that
many avoid by hitting the woods near its base.

Now that you've conquered the slide, you will need to over come the
false summit you are approaching. The woods are thick with trees
that have dead branches. These tend to bother hikers by poking and
prodding at you the entire length of the trip. There is a small view from
the false summit-you will be able to see the true summit from here.
Beware-the summit looks to be a very long distance away, it's really
only about a mile. From here you will descent slightly to the col to start
a strenuous climb to the summit ridge. The going is a little thick through
here but no down fall to really speak of. At about 0.2 miles from the
summit ridge the trees get shorter and much more like cripple bush.
Look back the way you came and you will notice your head is above the
trees and views are excellent. Continuing along the way, you will come

61

to a small bump just north-avoid it by staying to the right of its top. The top of this bump is thick with blow down and tightly woven trees. The summit from this part of the ridge is possibly the easiest stretch of the route, out side of the slide. The trees have mellowed out a little, and the ground underfoot is a little more stable.

Approx. distance from Monument Falls: 2.6 miles
Approx. time: 7 to 9 hours RT

Lower section of the Kilburn Slide

#53
Sawtooth #1
Elevation 3877'
Map #7

Sawtooth #1 is the highest peak in the Sawtooth Range; there are 4 others that make the list. Not all have views awaiting you, but #1 has some along the climb as well as from the summit. On another note, the Sawtooths have some of the wildest, densest and most challenging terrain in the northeast. When hiking in this range plan on going about a ½ mile an hour on average, a little faster in the lower reaches then to almost a dead crawl the higher up you get.

*Via Pine Pond Trail
*Trail/Bushwhack
*Green Route

This trail starts from the end of Averyville Road in Lake Placid. This spot was also the old starting point for the Northville/Placid Trail. At the end of Averyville Road is a dirt jeep road. Drive this to the parking area about 0.5 miles in. You can park here or take your chances driving a little further in with a high clearance 4-wheel drive vehicle. With our jeep, in dry conditions, we were able to drive in all the way to our bushwhack point. The Pine Pond Trail/Road has a few ups and downs and one "interesting" section of large rocks to drive over. Other sections are slightly flooded with mud puddles and an occasional log to drive over or around. We started 1.3 miles in along the road, which is an intersection with an old state access road. There is a sign forbidding motorized vehicle travel beyond a small chain. From here the road drops down to the shore of Cold Brook and crosses a very wet beaver dam, next to a gorgeous beaver pond. I've actually seen smaller lakes. There is an intersection not long after the pond. Just stay right and in fact always

Old tote road into the Sawtooth Range

stay right whenever you come to an intersection. The road then follows along the shore of the brook before climbing to a shelf. Now the hike is along a meandering old narrow road which will feel like a highway on the way out. The road ends on the side of the SE bump.

From the end of the road we continued along the col to another brook crossing, which was much easier than the first. We crossed directly over the brook and took a heading just W of S to hook up with a fork in the beginning of Cold Brook. There are numerous small ups and down along this section that are hidden between the contour lines of the map, making this a very long section indeed. You'll find a lot of consistent dead fall along the way as well, and it will slow the pace down quite a bit.

Once at the intersection of the brook, you'll discover that the brook is very open of debris and heavily covered in rocks. This makes for some good rock hoping. I would recommend this to anyone climbing the peak from this side. If the brook is low enough to stay in, do it as long as possible. We stayed in the brook up to about 2900' and 1.3 miles. Occasionally we had to take shore leave to get around a pool or slippery section, but quickly returned to the pleasant hike within. At around 2900' where we left the brook we came to a 50' waterfall which was breathtaking. Well worth stopping for a few photographs.

On the E shore of the brook there is a steep embankment that we scrambled up, using every piece of vegetation in the process. It's about a 70 degree pitch with loose and wet footing along the way, so some care is definitely a must. You will now be above the waterfall which is now behind you. A band of cliffs soon follows. Very cool, but avoidable to the right. There is a beautiful natural rock shelter here, one of those wonderful discoveries you'll find while bushwhacking.

The woods from here were open black spruce with little to no dead fall to climb over or go around, but you will pay for it with the occasional short sections of thicker stuff. The key here is to head E just a little to avoid it.

below the summit, and facing a section with a grade steep enough that it would turn you back if you could see the exposure and not have trees to aid you. The ground is covered in about 4-6 inches of really soft moss, cool to the touch but very unstable. The moss and small trees appear to be growing over smooth rock. It may have been a short steep slide that has completely overgrown.

The summit of Sawtooth #1 is amazing; you can feel the combination of solitude and kinship with the few who have climbed this peak. There are great views that take in the nearby Seward's to the distant Santanoni's and MacIntyre's. You can also see just how rugged this mountain range is and how thick the N sides of these peaks really are.

Approx. distance from parking at trailhead: 6.7 miles
Approx. distance from bushwhack point: 4 miles
Approx. distance from Pine Pond Trail intersection with woods road: 4.75 miles
Approx. time is 10 to 12 hours, RT-depending on which route you choose and how hot and humid and buggy it might be.

*Via Sawtooth #2
*Bushwhack
*Blue Route

This description is from Sawtooth #2 to Sawtooth #1 when doing a traverse over the two peaks.

From the summit of Sawtooth #2 head SE through some of the thickest forest in the northeast and descend very steeply 0.4 to the col. Along the descent you will see Sawtooth #1 as it appears closer and closer to you. Be very careful on this descent because the duff that covers the forest floor is very unstable and you may find yourself breaking through. It is another 0.6 miles of very steep, thick going from the col to the summit of Sawtooth #1.

Approx. distance from Sawtooth #2: 1 mile.
Approx. time between the summits: 1 to 2 hours. Good luck.

Fork in the brook on northern approach

View from Sawtooth #1

#54
Panther Mountain
Elevation 3865'
Map #5

 Panther Mountain has a few different choices for an approach, none of which are better than another. Panther was my 99th peak and I enjoyed every minute of the climb. Combined with Buell Mountain, it's a full day's adventure.

*Via the West
*Road/Bushwhack
*Green Route

This road is land leased by a local fish and game club and you should obtain permission before proceeding. The approach is a well used dirt road with a number of intersections on it. When you come to one, just remember to stay straight and take the one in the middle. If all else fails, check a GPS reading. The road climbs steadily but never to steep all the way to its height of land between Panther and Brown Pond Mountains. The length of the road to the col is 4.2 miles and climbs around 850'. The col is at about 2800' in elevation with only 900' feet of climbing to go, that elevation is gained in just 0.8 miles.

From the col turn just south of east and begin a steady climb to the top. The going is very open; in fact if one was so inclined they could almost climb to the summit and not touch a single piece of vegetation. The grade is steady for most of the distance with just a couple short, steep, spots near the summit crown. Unfortunately, Panther's summit is totally wooded with no real views to speak of. On our descent of Panther we came upon an old small slide on the W side. It's a beautiful spot with a couple small views from the top, please be careful it's very mossy and slippery.

Approx. distance from trailhead: 5 miles
Approx. time: 3 to 4 hours, one way

*Via Brown Pond Mountain
*Bushwhack
*Blue and Green Routes

This route is for the extended day hike and traverse from Brown Pond Mountain.

Coming from the summit of Brown Pond descends very steeply to the SW for 0.45 miles to the col with Panther. This descent is through relatively open woods, there is a little dead fall around the summit crown of Brown Pond, but very easy to avoid or climb over it if the mood strikes.

The descent starts off rather mellow before turning rather steep. At one point over 400' will be lost in a ¼ mile stretch. The last section to the col levels out before you cross the woods road that goes through the area. From here it's a short 0.8 miles to the summit. The woods are extremely open and enjoyable. As mentioned previously, Panther's wooded summit offers little opportunity for views, so take them in from the semi-open ledges you will encounter. For a more in depth look at the W side of Panther see the previous route description.

Approx. distance from Brown Pond Mountain: 1.3 miles
Approx. time: 1 to 1.5 hours

*Via Buell Mountain
*Bushwhack
*Black Route

This approach is from Buell Mountain, which can be approached via a bushwhack from the Snowy Mountain Trail, and an exit to the Sprague Pond Trailhead. Don't take this route to lightly, it's an all day adventure with a lot of off trail navigating in rarely visited forest. As you leave the Snowy Trail you will encounter private property and permission should be secured from the sportsman's club beforehand.

When leaving the summit of Buell head NE along the connecting ridge to Panther; then look for the property line and follow it NW along the ridge. The property line is an on and off again herd path and will lead you over the next small bump along the ridge; before fading out on the other side. The descent off of the bump is steep at first but moderates in a short distance. The woods are still very open, with a mixture of hardwoods and black spruce. Ahead is a very pronounced bump, one that should be skirted to stay out of the thicker woods. On our trip we skirted well below the top of this to the W. We circumnavigated until the ridge was again in front of us and Panther was easily seen to our left. From this side gaining access to the ridge was easy, and you can head right for it. The woods still very open, and the terrain quite easy to navigate. The climb to the summit ridge is a little steep from the W, but that will just get your heart pumping with anticipation of the top. The ridge is very easy to walk, with a couple small cliffs to skirt or climb through. The very top has a small cliff band that will need to be skirted to your right, but not too far. Panther's summit looks impressive from the Cedar River Road, but disappointing up close. The summit boasts nothing for views, but if you want seclusion, you've got it.

Approx. distance from Buell: 2+ miles
Approx. time: 2 to 2.5 hours, one way

#55
McKenzie Mountain
Elevation 3861'
Map #8

The McKenzie Wilderness is the area that you can find the other dominate peak that towers over Lake Placid. It also offers many great bushwhacks in addition to trails up smaller peaks. We'll cover the routes up McKenzie, as well as offering a traverse with its neighbor Moose Mountain which was covered earlier.

*Via Shore Owners Association Trail
*Trail
* Blue and Green Routes
The complete trail description for this route can be found in the Moose Mountain section of this guide (page 49).

From the trail junction along the SOA Trail that joins the Moose Mountain Trail it is a short distance to the summit of McKenzie. In fact it's less than 0.2 miles and 100' feet in elevation gain. This entire route is very well marked and lightly traveled-making a preferred route to the summit.

*Via Whiteface Inn Road (Jackrabbit Ski Trail)
*Trail
*Black Route
This is the shortest approach to this 3861' peak, and possibly the most popular. To find this trailhead, take the Whiteface Inn Road that leaves Rte 86 just W of the Village of Lake Placid. Continue for 1.5 miles, and you'll see the barricaded jeep trail on the left-the start of the trail.

The trail starts out as a jeep road then quickly turns into a cross country ski trail that ends on the McKenzie Pond Road near Saranac Lake. You won't have to hike this trail for that long of a distance. The old road begins a steady climb after only a short distance. It's quite rocky and at times wet, so a little bit of care is needed. At just over 0.25 mile a small road will come in on your left. This leads a 100 yards to a small dam, definitely worth a quick look. The trail continues to climb for another 0.4 miles before leveling off. At 1.5 miles from the trailhead you will come to a lean-to, a nice spot for a quick getaway. Soon after, you come to a usually reliable water source at a small brook that the trail crosses. Beyond and just under 2 miles is the junction with the trail from Rte 86.

At this 4 way junction take a right and finish the climb to the summit of McKenzie. The beginning has a tendency to be wet and quite slippery in spots, there are more wet spots than not. This trail has much erosion and is becoming wider in many places due to hikers avoiding wet spots and heavily eroded areas. Soon the real climb begins, becoming very steep in places. During one stretch of 0.4 miles you will pick up around 800' of elevation, before it levels out near a nice view point. Just beyond this is the top of the first of five summits of McKenzie Mountain- yes five. The second is only 0.2 miles from the first, then another 0.2 to the third. Take a breather here on a very nice ledge to the left of the trail. The fourth summit is 0.2 miles away with very little elevation lost up to this point. From here on you'll have to descend steeply into a col before the McKenzie summit. While you'll loose only around 100' of elevation, it will seem like more when you are there. The fifth and true summit is just beyond at another 0.4 miles. The best views are had from just before the summit from a ledge that faces NW to E.

Distance from the Whiteface Inn Road: 3.6 miles
Time: 4 to 5 hours RT

*Via Route 86
*Trail
*Red and Black Routes

This popular route is one of the longest, but none the less enjoyable. This route also passes by a smaller mountain named Haystack which offers more great views from the McKenzie Wilderness. To find the trailhead follow Rte. 86 out of Lake Placid toward Saranac Lake. The trailhead is marked and has a large parking area on the right side of the road.

The trail enters the woods and the trail register is shortly beyond, sign in and enjoy the climb. Soon after the register you will cross a small wet area and begin a short climb to the top of one of the many small knolls along the way. There are a couple of small brook crossings and at just less than 2 miles from the road; there is a small descent to the site of the old route that was closed some time back. After 0.65 miles of gradual climbing along the banks of Little Ray Brook you will come to the trail junction with Haystack Mountain-continue on to the right.

The trail is an old road and continues a slight climb for another mile before intersecting with the Jackrabbit Trail from the Whiteface Inn Road. The junction as well as the trail for the last part is usually very wet, no matter the weather. Continue straight ahead for the summit of McKenzie in another 1.75 miles: For the remaining trail description from this point see "Via Whiteface Inn Road" above.

Distance from Rte 86: 5.2 miles
Time: 5 to 6 hours RT

#56
Blue Ridge (Indian Lake)
Elevation 3860'
Map #9

 This particular Blue Ridge is the tallest of the four on the 100 Highest list, and possibly the toughest-at least by our findings. There are three routes up this peak, and by no means is one better than the other.

*Via Sucker Brook Trail
*Trail/Bushwhack
*Red Route

This trail is also an excellent approach for Lewey Mountain, but here it will be used for Blue Ridge. The Sucker Brook Trail is located off Rte 30 south of Indian Lake and north of Speculator. The start of the trail is just feet from the Lewey Lake State Campground Road.

The trail starts out flat and follows a lightly used path to an intersection with a dirt road that leads back to the campground. Keep to the right and then bear left at the next intersection by the trail register. The trail descends slightly to a wet area. Once across, this very lightly used trail is an extreme pleasure to walk. Although most of the time it is easy to follow, there are a few small sections that are overgrown. There are also a few sharp turns in the trail and small brook crossings that can be missed, so a little care and a sharp eye might be needed. The trail meanders along the 5.5 miles and many ups and downs, making the approach a workout on its own.

At around 5.5 mile you will come to drainage off from Blue Ridge that is the route to follow for a distance. Follow this brook for 0.75 miles keeping it to your left as much as possible before you leave its shores and follow the ridge to your right. The ridge starts out on a moderate but steady grade through open forest. At around 2800', the going becomes a steady steep at an ascent rate of about 100' for every 0.1 mile covered. The ridge will get noticeably steeper along the sides, as the climb gets very steep near the top. With the exception of a few small patches of firs, the woods up to this point aren't thick. These denser woods can usually be avoided with a short detour around them or looking for a clear shot through them. While downed trees aren't currently a problem, with the ever changing weather and a few harsh winters that could change overnight. After 1.4 miles of bushwhacking the summit is yours. The views are mostly obstructed, but with some exploring who knows what can be found. Most of the views you will enjoy are along the steeper portions of the bushwhack.

Approx. distance from trailhead: 6.9 miles
Approx. time: 8 to 10 hours RT

*Via Old Military Road
*Trail/Bushwhack
*Blue Route

This route is a little shorter but involves more bushwhacking, the call is yours.

The Pillsbury Mountain Trailhead is also located off Rte 30 south of Indian Lake but closer to Speculator. Look for Perkins Clearing Road (dirt road) to join Rte 30 on the W side. Follow here to a T intersection at Perkins Clearing, go right. The road will soon cross the Miami River and come to another intersection referred to as Sled Harbor. Going straight is now Old Military Road follow here to the gate and the trailhead. Old Military is a very rough section of road and some low clearance vehicles may not be able to continue. If you park your car at Sled Harbor, it's only a short walk up to the trailhead.

The trail section of this route is actually the continuance of Old Military Road. You will need to follow this old road for 1.9 miles to a footbridge.

The road is very easily traveled and should be a quick walk to the start of the bushwhack. Once across the foot bridge enter the woods and head NE up the ridge. This climb to the first bump along the ridge is open and relatively easy over a moderately easy grade, and at 0.6 miles you're on top of the first of many bumps. The second is just less than 0.2 miles away. The climb to the third bump is much more of a challenge, with the woods closing in a little and the grade getting a little steeper. The views from behind will take your mind off the effort. The fourth bump is just a small nub 0.2 miles away, it can be avoided rather easily to its right. The wood tightens up even more over the last 0.5 miles to the summit, but the views keep popping up in the nicest places-making for a great excuse for a break. Then at just over 2 miles from the bridge you're on the summit, enjoying lunch and the sound of only the breeze in the trees around you.

Approx. Distance from the trailhead: 4 miles
Approx. time: 6 to 7 hours RT

*Via Freemont Brook
*Bushwhack
*Green Route

Perkins clearing road is what you want to follow to a height of land where a small camping area is in the right. The old Callahan Brook Trail is located at the back of the camping area. The trail starts out a little wet along a slight down grade. There are a few trees to climb over and the trail is lightly marked with ribbon, but all in all pretty straight forward. Along this trail you will come to a fork, take the left fork to the brook and cross it over a downed tree just north of a beaver pond. The ground will look marshy but it's actually a soft grassy area that will bring you to the actual crossing of the Miami River. It sounds worse than it really is. In normal conditions the Miami River is only about 20' across and can easily be waded in many spots. Keep in mind it was during a small dry spell when we crossed, rain can easily change things making the Miami River faster and deeper.

Once across, bear right until you come to either a lightly flagged Callahan Trail again or Freemont Brook. Freemont is the brook you want to follow if you can't pick up or lose the Callahan Trail. For here, 80% of the Callahan Trail is easy to follow the other 20% is stop and look for the next ribbon. The woods are very open along this entire route up the brook, so if you do loose the trail, no big deal-just keep Freemont Brook on your right. Keep your eye open for a piece of an old stove that has a tree growing around it about 7 feet off the ground. Who knows how long ago this was placed in the crotch of a tree, or did the tree grow up around it as a sapling? One may never know.

Miami River Crossing

At about 2700' in elevation along the brook there will be a distinctive split rock-this is the point in which you need to leave the brook and head W up the very steep slopes of Blue Ridge.

Located someplace on this side of the mountain there is a crash site of an old C-46 transport plane from World War II. It crashed in September of 1944 on a training mission to Watertown. Second Lt. William R. Barohn; Second Lt. Charles G. Pate; T/Sgt. Edward V. Paska, were the three airmen who perished that foggy night in the lonely foothills of Hamilton County. On the wing a memorial was placed for those three airmen. We visited this site on our trip up Blue Ridge, but out of respect for the airmen of flight 115, and their families-I have left out the exact location of the crash site. Please feel free to explore on your own.

If you find the site and once the reality of it has worn off, you will need to start hiking up the steep slopes again toward the start of the ridge. Once atop the first bump of the ridge, take a second to catch your breath and take in some outstanding views from the steep slopes below. Your best option is to head directly over the ridge, it's pretty open with a lot of clear shots, and the only thick section is closer to the summit, about 50 feet below. The actual summit has no views, but a few could be had around the edges.

Approx. distance from parking: 4.5 miles
Approx. time: 7 to 8 hours RT

#57
North River Mountain
Elevation 3860'
Map #10

This peak has possibly one of the nicest and wildest views of the Adirondack 100 highest. One of the best approaches, however, is over private land leased by a sportsman's club. We can't strongly-enough suggest that you obtain permission or join before even thinking about the following the route.

*Via Cheney Cobble
*Bushwhack
*Blue Route

Well all I can say about this ridge traverse is, OUCH! No really, this has got to be one of the toughest sections out there. We headed off the summit with much confidence after touching the summit of Cheney Cobble in just about 2 hours from the car. That confidence lasted about 10 minutes.

From the summit there is an initial cliff that guards this side of the mountain. Once off that we only had to deal with thick woods, hidden holes, blow down, slippery terrain, thorn bushes, and the occasional small cliff. Avoid Cheney's sub-summit at all costs. You may be tempted as we were to go over it, thinking it would make the traverse shorter or to avoid a side hill hike-but it's much worse up there. We avoided it all together on a tip from fellow hikers who made the mistake.

The traverse was kind of strange in ways. One minute we would find ourselves almost falling off a small cliff, the next minute beating back almost impenetrable growth of evergreens, to a spot of openness that we hoped would last forever. It never did. By the time we got to the base

80

of North River we were all feeling the strain of what we had just been through. Our arms and legs burned from the scratches we received in just 0.75 miles, and we were not yet to the summit.

In the col the woods were very open and the climb from here looked to be much mellower along a steeper approach. It was a very pleasant hike from here; just a small section of thicker spruce slowed us down near the summit crown of North River. The views were outstanding just as they were from Cheney. From North River's summit it seemed as though most of the 100 highest could be seen; hard to believe? We could see Snowy in Indian Lake; does that make it more believable?

Approx. distance from Cheney Cobble: 1.1 miles, good luck.
Approx. time: 1.5 to 2 hours, one way

*Via the North
*Bushwhack
*Green Route

This route starts near the end of the private access road, we got permission to use and we utilized it for our descent after a traverse from Cheney Cobble. You will be reading this as a descent route, follow it in reverse if you wish to climb this way.

We left the summit of North River about an hour and 2 peanut butter and jelly sandwiches later, for what we expected to be a 1.5 mile "death march". However, off trail this term takes an all new meaning, because marching we were not. We had all reached our "tree quota" for the day- as my good friend, Tim, said so appropriately. This quota made further bushwhacking turn into us begging for it to end.

The initial woods from the summit started out very thick and very steep. The footing was nice and soft with no hidden holes, which was nice for a change. The woods became fairly open along the ridge down to the fork of Dudley Brook and this slightly lifted our tired spirits. Once in the col we were very pleased to find ferns

View from North River Mountain

started earlier that day. Engrossed in fun conversation, the hike out passed by rather quickly, finding ourselves uplifted every time we came to an open patch of woods. But most of the hike along the brook was just one tree after another that exceeded our "quota" for the day. Nothing terribly thick, but every branch seemed to have it in for us. Roughly 0.25 to 0.5 miles from the road we came upon an old logging road, which delivered us back to our cars. We could have used that long before.

Back at the car we joked, talked and refueled, but without saying so, we all felt great about what we accomplished.

Approx. distance from the private road: 1.7 miles
Approx. time: 4 to 5 RT
Approx. distance as a loop with Cheney Cobble: 5.25 miles
Approx. time for loop: 9 to 10 hours

#58
Sentinel Mountain
Elevation 3838'
Map #11

This is yet another peak in the 23,000 acre Sentinel Wilderness. While it's the one the range is named after, it's only the second highest of the four that reside here. Just like the other 3, it's a challenge to summit, with its thick canopy fighting off the brave.

*Via Liscomb Brook from the East
*Bushwhack
*Black Route

This is by far the shortest approach to the summit, and the quickest. That, however, doesn't mean easy. Start by driving up the Bartlett Road just outside of Upper Jay; park along the road after 2.7 miles, not far after a sharp left turn. Right in this area you will notice an old logging road now grassed over by time-this is the start of the journey. Follow this old road to near its end somewhere near where it veers from the brook. The road is very nice with very few obstacles to slow you down. The road doesn't last long- only around 0.75 miles. From here you will need to make a bearing W toward the summit of Sentinel. The woods aren't too bad at first, with hardwoods surrounding you, only the new growth slowing things down a bit. Ever been slapped in the face by a springy branch of a 1 inch sapling? Once you do, you'll see what I mean.

The brook falls dry after 1 mile from the road and just under 1000 feet in elevation change. From here it is a short 1.1 miles to the summit. The terrain gets much steeper and the woods thicker. You'll experience taller spruce, with sharp pointed dead branches that are waist to face height. Sunglasses would be a nice addition to your pack for this little climb.

Soon you will find yourself along a ridge that seems to last forever. Along most of the ridge you will wonder if you had passed the summit at some point, but you haven't. Soon the true summit will become apparent as a small nubble along the end of the ridge. It is very thick along this ridge, and even more so the closer to the summit you get. Don't be surprised to find yourself arm wrestling with tree branches, you won't win. Just find a way around if you need to. The summit will surprise you, it's small, room for about 3 hikers, and the trees are short. There are pretty decent views of Whiteface to the MacIntyre Range, as well as numerous other high peaks.

Approx. distance from Bartlett Road: 2 miles
Approx. time: 6.5 to 8 hours RT

*Via The Cobble Mountain
*Bushwhack
*Red Route

This approach starts from the same area, but doesn't follow the old road. This is not a preferred route but one that would open up another possibility with outstanding views.

From the sharp turn on the Bartlett Road-as mentioned in the above description-enter the woods and cross Liscomb Brook, and head NE. The woods are very open along this entire trip to the base of The Cobble. From the base to the summit you will find it to be a little thicker with a couple small patches of blow down to maneuver. The summit of Cobble is only just over 0.5 miles from the road and less than 1 hour away. The entire top is surrounded by cliffs with open views from all around, a real gem.

The ridge to Sentinel runs west along a semi-open ridge. After a small descent and a little longer climb you will top off on another small bump along the ridge, where there are a couple view spots.

Summit party on Sentinel Mountain

The remaining climb along the ridge is fairly uneventful, just the occasional blow down patch, sections of thicket-you know the typical 100 Highest barriers. Just beware along this route, the ground is very unstable and you'll find yourself punching holes through the duff along the way. I don't recommend returning this way when a more direct descent to the car is available. That is unless you want to soak up a few more views. Follow the previous route above in reverse for a direct route to your car.

Approx. distance from Bartlett Road: 2.6 miles
Approx time: 6 to 8 hours RT

Sentinel's summit as seen from the ridge

#59
Lyon Mountain
Elevation 3830'
Map #12

Lyon Mountain is the farthest north of any other of the peaks in the Adirondack 100 Highest. That provides this mountain it's own distinction and viewpoint. Not many mountains can say they offer an international view. Along this wide open summit sits an old abandoned fire tower, still worthy of a climb to the cab to take in its expansive views. With help from the DEC the tower is planned as one to be saved and has recently been repainted. It is now awaiting its new rails, steps and floor boards. But, is deemed totally safe to climb

*Via Averill Peak
*Bushwhack
*Red Route

This is a short bushwhack from Lyon's next door neighbor, Averill. Averill is the only other ADK 100 Highest peak in the vicinity. For a route description see "Averill via Lyon Mountain" in the Averill Peak chapter of this guide (page 101).

*Via Chazy Lake Road
*Trail
*Blue Route

The trail to this summit starts from the Chazy Lake Road. Chazy Lake Road is 3.5 miles E of the Village of Lyon Mountain, off Rte 374. Follow Chazy Lake Road for just under 2 miles, the dirt access road for the trail will be on the right. In winter the trail starts here, being unmaintained during that time of year it will be impassable by vehicle. During other seasons, you can drive the 0.9 miles to the end, which is the site of the old ski area lodge. The trail is to the left of the ruins. The trail starts climbing almost immediately. You'll first follow an old jeep road that enters the woods along a never ending rocky surface. The grade isn't to steep at first. You will cross a few wet areas, an exposed culvert, but mostly loose rocks. Not long into the hike the trail turns from a moderate climb to a relentlessly steep one. Footing at times needs to be properly planned, especially on the descent. After 1.25 miles of climbing, you'll come to the site of the old observer's cabin, only parts of the foundation and the stairs remain. After an extremely steep section the going levels out along the ridge. Soon the summit and fire tower are reached.

There are great views from Lyon's summit rocks, but much more can be seen from the cab of the tower itself. You can look over the High Peaks to the S, Lake Champlain and the Green Mountain of Vermont to the E, and on a very clear day, the White Mountains of New Hampshire and the faint skyline of Montreal.

Distance from Chazy Lake Road: 2.5 miles
Approx time: 3 to 4 hours RT

Summit of Lyon Mountain

#60
Sawtooth #2
Elevation 3820'
Map #13

 Sawtooth #2 sits just west of its higher sister, Sawtooth #1. The summit consists of two almost identical knobs; on the maps they look to be the same height. Even though there are no extra contour lines showing, the western peak is slightly higher.

*Via Sawtooth #1
*Bushwhack
*Blue Route
This short bushwhack is used when traversing the two peaks. For a description see the Sawtooth #1 section in this guide (page 63).

*Via the Pine Pond Trail
*Trail/Bushwhack
*Green and Red
Follow the same route as you would for Sawtooth #1,see Sawtooth #1 via Pine Pond Trail in the appropriate section of this guide (page 63).

Once you are on the brook that flows from the col between Sawtooths #1 and #2 you will need to follow it upstream about as far as the approach for #1. At around 2900' or 1/3 mile from the col, head west to the first of the two bumps, only 0.4 miles away. The best method of travel from here is simply a matter of how hard can you push. The forest seems to have weaved a most evil web; unfortunately you need to go through it. Alright it's not that bad, but you'll have some scratches when you go to sleep that evening. You will climb just under 780 feet in those

0.4 miles. It's not an unimaginable steep but a relentless one given the thickness of the woods around you. That's just part of the game in the Sawtooth Range. The views are quite nice from this eastern peak, some of the nicest in the range, so take time to enjoy them. From here it's just a short jaunt of 0.15 miles to the second bump, if you decide you want to go over there. You will only loose about 20' between the two summits, and the going is nothing worse than what you've experienced so far. But it's pretty obvious which one is higher from where you are standing.

Approx. distance from parking: 7.25 miles
Approx. time: 11 to 12 hours RT

*Via Ward Brook Trail
*Trail/Bushwhack
*Black Route

The Ward Brook Trail starts from the Corey's Road, which is located off Rte 3 between the Villages of Tupper Lake and Saranac Lake. The trail itself is maintained, so besides being muddy during the wet season, it's a relatively easy access to the bushwhack. Once you're on the truck trail follow it left to a brook crossing, climb the small hill, and this is the start of the bushwhack.

This is the same start as for Sawtooth #4. As you climb be sure to avoid the small bump that sits on the slopes of #4, by skirting it to the NW. The woods through here are not too bad as far as being thick, but there is a lot of scattered dead fall that will need to be skirted and stepped over. This slows down the pace quite a bit.

Once you've passed the small bump you will find that the lay of the land is much better. The woods are more open and the terrain quite a bit flatter. In here you may notice a few game paths that lead in the direction you want to go which is E toward the brook. In seemingly no time you will be resting on the rocks that cover this gorgeous stream.

The best approach from here, we found out, is to keep the brook in sight and follow it to about 2700' which is its source. From here you can take your heading E toward the summit of #2. The woods through here are very nice-not completely open-but very easy to navigate. We used this

Sewards from Sawtooth #2 (notice the human pin cushion)

as a descent route, and decided that it would make an excellent ascent route as well. Climbing straight up from the brook at lower elevations will bring you to a very tall cliff band, with trees that are thicker than anything imaginable. The true summit will be the one to the W, which so happens to be the one on your bearing. You can venture over to the other, but it is clearly lower than the one you will be standing on.

Sawtooth #2's summit has some of the best views in the Adirondacks, offering a more unique perspective than those from many of the High Peaks. There isn't much room on the summit for more than a couple people, so you'll have to take turns with the views. Did you remember your camera?

Approx. distance from trailhead: 7.5 miles
Approx. time: 10 to 12 hours RT

The brook up the north side of the Sawtooth Range

Sunny "The Wonder Dog" on Sawtooth #2

#61
TR Mountain
Elevation 3820'
Map #14

TR Mountain is located just NW of Indian falls, a mere 0.25 miles off the VanHovenburg Trail. The summit is not named on many maps, but on some the summit is noted by a triangle, marking it as a Adirondack 100 Highest peak. Originally referred to as "Unnamed Peak Indian falls" in trail guides it now has the name TR-short for Theodore Roosevelt. This previously unnamed peak was renamed in the 90's by Governor George Pataki in recognition of one of the Governor's favorite President. Teddy Roosevelt happened to love exploring and hiking in the Adirondacks and legend has it that he was informed that he was the new President of the United States while traveling on a carriage road that is now called Route 73. There is a large boulder commemorating this event in a small pull off area of route 73 near the Cascade Lakes, called Stagecoach Rock.

*Via the VanHovenburg Trail
*Trail/Herd Path
*Red Route

To climb TR Mountain, start from the Adirondack Loj. The Loj is located at the very end of the Adirondack Loj Road, which is E of the Village of Lake Placid. The trail is located at the back of the parking lot and leads you 2.3 miles to Marcy Dam. The trail to the dam is very busy and will be the quickest section of the hike. From Marcy Dam you will need to follow the heavily used trail to Mount Marcy. As the trail continues it begins to get much rockier, which slows the pace a little. The next trail junction is for Phelps Mountain, ignore this and continue straight. Shortly beyond you will cross a bridge over Phelps Brook-this is where the real climbing begins. The route starts about 0.5 mile from the bridge crossing. It is at the top of the steep hill along a flatter area. The herd path is located just in the woods. It's not noticeable from the trail, and may take a little looking around. However, once you find it, it's very easy to follow. You will find the path to be well cut through the forest; the tread is well eroded on the steep sections. Just before the summit there is a patch of blowdown which makes the path indiscernible, climb over the half dozen downed trees and the trail will again appear. Not far past there and just upon the ridge is the best view, a small opening looking toward Tabletop.

The summit is stomped down a little, but still offers no views. Just beyond the summit a downed tree is all you will have to help you with a view. Mount Colden is the most prominent peak in view. I suggest climbing this peak in winter. The added feet of snow make for much better views.

Approx. distance from the Loj: 4.3 miles
Approx. time: 5 to 6 hours RT

TR Mountain from Indian Falls

*Via the NW Ridge
*Trail/Bushwhack
*Blue Route

This route again starts from the Adirondack Loj and follows the VanHovenburg Trail. After you leave the Marcy Dam area and head up the trail toward Mount Marcy you will shortly come to a spot where the trail crosses Phelps Brook-first on a low water route, then a high water route. This is the where we started our approach to get to the ridge. There is a faint sign of an old path that starts along the right hand side of the stream, but slowly fades out as it heads up hill. The next 0.4 miles is rather moderate through a semi-open forest, on a thick layer of duff. The remaining climb to the first bump along the ridge is much steeper with 650' elevation change in just over 0.25 miles. The first summit is reached without to much blowdown getting in the way but further progress up the ridge is a different story.

When you're on the ridge itself, you will quickly notice a combination of old blowdown and new blowdown mixed with new growth. This combination makes for very slow progress and you should plan on at least an hour to navigate the next 0.50 miles to the summit. We found it easier to walk along the downed trees in spots, rather than try and go around or under them. The climb along the ridge is rather moderately pitched with no cliffs to skirt and make you trip that much more difficult. The wooded summit sits at 3820' towering over Indian Falls.

Approx. distance from the Loj: 4 miles
Approx. time: 5.5 to 6 hours RT

#62
Averill Peak
Elevation 3810'
Map #12

 This peak is found just south of its sister, Lyon Mountain, and not coincidentally, in the Town of Lyon Mountain. Averill sticks out like a sore thumb in the horizon with a radio tower standing on its shoulder. The main route up this peak is over private land that passes through a gravel pit area. The gate is no longer closed and many local ATV riders use the area for 4-wheeling. So, public access may not even be an issue anymore. Be careful of leaving your vehicle inside the gate. There is a sign that says it's closed and locked at the end of the work day. If this sign is still valid, is unsure.

*Via Tower Access Road
*Trail/Bushwhack
*Green Route

Finding Averill is sometimes harder than doing the hike. You will need to navigate the local road system. From Route 374 in the Village of Lyon Mountain look for Standish Road and follow it for approximately 1 mile, to a road that enters from the left. The road is rough and passes through a tight knit community of houses. On the left of the road you will notice a large pile of mining dust, with usually many tracks from local ATV riders. Here, following the side road around to the left and up a small hill, until you come to a once gated area. (I say once, because it has never been closed when I have been there, and no activity in the area is noticed). You will need to park outside the gate along the roadside and walk through the area.

On your left will be the top of the large pile of mining dust, and on the right is a run down storage building. Continue on along the dirt road as it passes by a few smaller piles of rubble. When it splits, continue to the right. After only five minutes or so from your car the road will follow a power line then end near a power shed. From here continue to follow the power line, now along an ATV trail. This portion will take you all the way to the communication tower, which you could see from the road. The trail is very easy to follow and climbs very moderately for the first half of the route. The route is very muddy in spots and tends to be a great breading ground for mosquitoes and deer flies. Approximately 0.75 miles from the tower, the trail begins to get steep and at times slippery. Once at the tower site, the actual summit of Averill Peak is uphill to your left (East).

While the summit is only 0.4 of a mile away, you'll have to fight your way through some fairly thick spots to get views and gain elevation. The route you are on continues over the ridge, but you will want to exit just past the tower and fight your way through the thick growth that lines the trail. Once through the thickest section, the woods open up a little to offer you short sections of clear areas, which look like trampled areas of old herd paths or areas where deer have bedded down. This could be possible because Averill does get a little traffic from the locals and people bagging The Adirondack 100 Highest. The exact summit has amazing views along a short band of cliffs.

Approx. distance from gate: 3 miles
Approx. time: 3 to 4 hours RT

*Via Lyon Mountain
*Bushwhack
*Red Route

This short bushwhack could be used as a loop, when a second car is parked on the other side. For a brief trail description see Lyon Mountain via Chazy Lake Road in the Lyon Mountain chapter of this guide (page 88).

I had heard a rumor of a herd path from Lyon toward Averill, so we went looking for it. Sure enough, just over the summit rock of Lyon is a wide open herd path. It is lightly marked with erratic shaped clear plastic markers. Very soft underfoot we were enjoying the fact we weren't going to have to bushwhack the entire ridge. The path leads us to a cleared dirt road on the shoulder of Lyon. We followed the road left in hopes that we would see where the herd path continues, all while hoping it still did. At the end of the road to the left, about 200 feet, the path continues behind a small rock cairn. From here the path continues softly to an amazing lookout toward Averill. There is a faint arrow painted on the rock to the left. From here the herd path is very tricky. Only faint red blazes on sporadic trees leads the way toward Averill Peak. We followed the path as best we could, until we lost it totally in wilds of the col.

The col is a wide very flat area, open with tiny soft evergreens. At the back of the flat area is a wall of thick evergreens lined up like hedges in a straight line in both directions. The ridge we needed to follow was behind this. We found our way around to the left in hopes of obtaining the ridge without to much of a struggle. The woods are quite a mess through this section, thick, wet, dead, and very unstable. But the closer we got to the ridge the more open the terrain became. Only a short section before the initial bump along the ridge was a challenge, worthy of a few scratches. In fact this section ate a Black Diamond trekking pole, so, if you see it, can you grab it for us? Thanks!

Once on the initial first bump we were back in the open, enjoying the fact that we weren't getting beat up. But we still had a couple other small bumps along the way before the summit of Averill would be below our feet. The next bump was a jagged looking one, from our angle. Standing at the base of it, we could see why. It has quite a ring of cliffs around it, nothing to huge however. There is a herd path around the left of them, which exited us out on the top. On the summit of this amazing little knob is probably the best view of the ridge; a long open ledge, steep drop off, and no trees in the way.

At this point there is only one small bump in the way. It's wooded, but very open, with small paths through the thicker sections. We obtained the trail just shy of 0.2 miles from the actual summit of Averill.

Approx. distance from Lyon Mountain: 1.3 miles
Approx. time: 1.5 to 2 hours, one way
Approx. loop distance: 6.8 miles
Approx. time for loop: 8 to 9 hours

Moss carpet in route to Averill from Lyon Mountain

#63
Avalanche Mountain
Elevation 3800'
Map #14

Avalanche Mountain sits in the valley between Algonquin and Colden, and from Marcy Dam it can be picked out quite easily. The first explorers of the area found this peak to be a problem child. It's sheer cliffs blocked off access to Avalanche Pass, Lake Colden, and the country beyond. This slight problem made them change their route and make passage through Caribou Pass, which happens to be one of the routes we use today to climb Avalanche Mountain.

*Via Caribou Pass
*Trail/Bushwhack
*Blue Route

This route is more bushwhack than trail work, once you leave the state trail. First start your hike from the Adirondack Loj and hike the 2.3 miles into Marcy Dam. From Marcy Dam follow the trail that leads to Avalanche Pass. Stay on this trail for 0.7 miles to the herd path for Kagel Lean-to. From the lean-to follow the brook down stream for about 0.1 miles to where Wright Brook enters on the opposite side. Pick up Wright Brook and follow it through Caribou Pass. Be sure to keep the brook to your right, there is an old trail that follows this side, even though intermittent, it will get you close to the height of land in the pass.

You will see that at first the trail is a little hard to pick up, but quickly it will become clear as day. Many spots are very muddy, but only a few spots slow down the pace because of blowdown. The old trail slowly climbs through open forest, at some times close to the brook, then others times it wanders away. When it does the brook is always an ear shot away. Occasionally the trail will disappear totally, but if you look around it's usually only feet away. However, you don't want to depend on this trail to get you to your exit point, keeping the brook to your right will.

After a little over a mile of following the brook and trail, you will need to take a bearing S and head somewhat steeply up hill. The woods here are fairly open, with only a couple small sections of thick spruce. Before to long the grade gets steeper and you're in an all out scramble to the summit. The woods are still very open, but the ground is much more unstable with small ledges to surmount or skirt. These small cliffs, however, open up some great views of the cirque on Wright, and add nice places to break-up the climbing.

This route will bring you to the summit ridge, where there is a short; thick bushwhack of 0.2 miles to the partially open summit. The top of Avalanche provides some great views of the entire area. They're not all in one place, but if you look, you'll find them. You'll be looking up at the scars on Colden and the Trap Dike, a route that so many people use to get to the summit of Mount Colden. If you look in the opposite direction, you can see Wright and Algonquin towering above.

The descent is now in your hands, do you return via Caribou Pass, or follow the ridge down to Avalanche Lean-to? The ridge description follows.

Approx. distance from Loj: 4.1 miles
Approx. time: 6 to 7 hours RT

Colden from Ridge Route up Avalanche Mountain

*Via ridge from the NE
*Bushwhack
*Green Route

This way seems to be the more popular route to the summit, I have yet to see why. The going is much thicker, and the ascent isn't any less. You'll again start your day from the Adirondack Loj, hike into Marcy Dam, follow the trail leading to Avalanche Pass, but stop at the intersection with the Avalanche Pass Trail and the Lake Arnold Trail. This was the site of the old Avalanche Lean-to this is where the bushwhack starts.

The terrain starts our moderate through open woods. Before to long the landscape changes by becoming steeper, and thicker balsam and spruce start to move in. Once on the main ridge the climb moderates and views of Colden and the MacIntyre's start to pop up. You'll see that the best views are from the small sub-summits along the ridges.

The downfall, though, is that the summits are pretty thick around the edges. After another 0.6 miles of climbing there is a small descent off a small cliff that will have to be negotiated. The last section of climbing is up the main summit that has been in and out of your sights for so long. You'll encounter an interesting little high altitude marshy area, and then down another small ledge. Just below the summit there is an open area that appears to lead down into Caribou Pass. This is where the Caribou Pass route intersects the ridge if you have a loop in mind. The summit awaits only feet away now on a small knob.

Approx. distance from the Loj: 4 miles
Approx. time: 6 to 7 hours RT
Approx. loop distance: 8.1 miles
Approx. loop time: 6 to 8 hours

#64
Buell Mountain
Elevation 3786'
Map #5

Buell can be done by itself, from two directions or combined with other 100 Highest to make for a much longer day in the woods. One of my favorite peak bagging trips I've ever been on is a loop over Snowy's ridge to Buell, then to Panther, over to Brown Pond and out. When combining these two routes, the one up Panther from the Brown Pond Mountain, and the one up Brown from Wakely Dam, the complete trip are around 12 miles and a full day of hiking in a quiet open forest. A good portion of this range you are hiking in is over private land leased by hunting clubs. Please obtain permission before following these routes.

*Via Panther Mountain
*Bushwhack
*Black Route
See Panther via Buell in the Panther Mountain chapter of this guide (page 71).

*Via the Snowy Mountain Trailhead
*Trail/Bushwhack
*Blue and Red Routes
This route starts off Rte 30 south of Indian Lake, and follows the Snowy Mountain Trail to around 2450' (for trail information about Snowy see the Snowy Mountain chapter in this guide, page 56). The bushwhack begins around 2450' where the trail crosses the brook for the last time. You will now be crossing private land, please get permission.

A semi open forest awaits you and follows the brook up the shoulder to the ridge. The ridge is about 0.6 miles from the trail and nearly 500' of climbing. If you keep yourself close to the edge of the ridge on the right of the brook, you'll come upon an old logging road that will bring you to the top of the ridge in a small valley. If you fail to intersect the old road just take a heading for the small valley and you will find it there.

The descent into Squaw Valley is an easy one especially if you've found the woods road. The descent down the road is very easy to follow, but is very wet and slippery during most seasons. It will lead you to Squaw Brook in Squaw Valley…go figure. From the floor of the valley you will come upon a well used dirt road. Follow this road left for about 100-150 yards to a small sand pit. At the top of this sand pit is another old logging road. It's pretty overgrown in sections but still easy to follow. You will then cross a decent size brook after a short distance. Continue on to the second major brook crossing, leave the road and start bushwhacking toward the summit of Buell (NW). The woods are very open, with very little to get in your way. There are fields of ferns and fields of grass scattered along the entire route up, in fact I don't remember getting a scratch on us all the way up.

Near the summit you will however encounter some ledges that could be a blast to work your way through. Do to a late start and a warm day; we skirted most of them to save time by keeping the really steep sections of cliffs to our left. You can play with the cliffs or move to the right where we followed what looked to be an old woods road and/or game path. This led us close to the ridge. The ledges here inviting and were calling our name-so we attacked the last small set. All I can say is this terrain is some of the steepest stuff I've ever encountered. While all the cliffs can be avoided this is still an extremely steep section of terrain where using your hands are necessary. Buell's summit views are disappointing, but from the tops of the ledges some small views can be had back toward Snowy and the southern peaks.

Approx. distance from the trailhead: 4.5 miles
Approx. time: 3 to 4 hours, one way

Buell Ridge from Snowy Ridge

```
(1 @ 0.
Solid Milk Bar
 9780641810459              TI
 (1 @ 2.95) Member Card 10% (0.30)
 (1 @ 2.65)                          2

Subtotal                            57.79
Sales Tax T1 (8.000%)                4.62
TOTAL                               62.41
MASTERCARD DEBIT                    62.41
 Card#:  XXXXXXXXXXXXX8114

MEMBER SAVINGS                       6.44


           Thanks for shopping at
              Barnes & Noble

V101.13                   07/20/2008  06:43PM
```

CUSTOMER COPY

#65
Boreas Mountain
Elevation 3776'
Map #15

Boreas Mountain once had a state trail that lead to the summit, the home of fire towers past. But since the removal of the tower all DEC signs of the trail have been removed. The only trail that climbs Boreas is a private one, maintained by the Elk Lake Lodge. You may use this route only as a guest of the lodge.

*Via the Elk Lake Lodge Trail
*Trail
*Blue Route

Please get permission to use this route, so that it doesn't cause problems with the land owners and the public easement that the state has with Elk Lake Lodge property.

Start from the parking area near the lodge and cross the road as though you were going to Panther Gorge. This state trail descends all the way to the valley below before crossing the brook. The trail will soon intersect with a dirt road that you will need to follow to the left. This road soon crosses a wooded bridge and goes straight over a small hill. You will notice the state trail leaves the road on the right before the top of the hill. Don't follow the trail; the road is the route to Boreas.

About a half mile or so down the road you will see an old sign that points to Boreas. There are a few ups and downs along the route, in fact more downs initially, then a lot of up. The road ends once it reaches the brook that the trail once followed. From here you will need to ford the brook and follow the trail to the summit. The trail starts out rather mellow, but steady up to the old site of the caretakers cabin. This spot is easily

111

noticeable by the obvious cleared area. From here the trail gets quite steep all the way to the summit. Footing is rather easy, but a couple breaks along the way are defiantly in order. The summit offers some views off toward the Dix Range and back toward Elk Lake. Signs of the old fire tower are still apparent. The cement footings and tie down loops are visible. A benchmark marks the top.

Approx. distance from the trailhead: 3.2 miles
Approx. time: 4 to 5 hours, RT

Blue Mountain in winter

#66
Blue Mountain
Elevation 3760'
Map #16

On really busy days in the summer you'll often find yourself sharing the summit with dozens of other people. You may at times having to wait your turn to climb the tower, like you were at an amusement park waiting to ride a roller coaster. However it is well worth the wait, many small rock outcropping will give you views while you're waiting. But you won't have to worry about that in the winter. Even though this is a very popular climb in the winter, the chances of a backed up line are very unlikely. For one; the wind and icy steps of the tower often turn back all but the truly dedicated, and trips to the top flight are very short and sweet.

*Via Blue Mountain Trail
*Trail
*Blue Route
The trailhead is off Rte 28 in Blue Mountain Lake just 0.1 miles up the hill from the Adirondack Museum-the trailhead and ample parking will be on the right. On the left of the parking lot is the trailhead for Tirrell Pond, the one you want is at the back of the parking area near the register. I describe this as a winter climb, because it is most enjoyed during that time of year.

Once you've signed in you will enter the woods and cross a frozen stream and start the first leg of your climb. Climbing now for 20 minutes you will cross a couple icy areas where a couple streams meander off the side of the mountain across the trail. The trail now levels off for a short time before climbing steadily again to 1.4 miles where you can get another short breather.

At this point, the real climbing begins, and ice makes a more prominent appearance. The trail is now over rock slab; some spots bare, some with snow, some with very slick waterfall ice. Oh yeah, black ice too. Even though the footing is tricky this 0.5 mile is very enjoyable. The spruce that line both sides of the trail, give this a feeling of a tree lined tunnel, and with the massive amounts of snow this area gets-the weight of the snow closes the opening in around you. The remaining few hundred yards of this route are along the flat ridge, where you'll find yourself looking above the tree tops for the tower. Trust me you'll look.

The Blue Mountain Trail when not frozen

The summit is flat and very often wind blown. In winter, the once silver colored tower is now white with rime ice. Just over the summit is the observer's cabin and over head are all the lines from the radio tower, all of which are now painted white. The views range from nearby Tirrell Pond to the distant High Peaks Region. Many more frozen ponds and lakes as well as snowcapped summits fill the horizon-you'll just have to go see for yourself. It's a beautiful scene, one for which you will remember for a lifetime.

Round trip distance: 4 miles
Round trip time: 3 to 4 hours, in winter

*Via Tirrell Pond Trail
*Trail
*Green Route

This route starts along a state trail but veers off and follows a jeep road to the summit. The road is private and you should seek permission to use it ahead of time. It can make for a nice one car loop.

Starting from the same trailhead parking, look to the left side and you'll see the trailhead to Tirrell Pond-follow it. The trail parallels the road along a fairly flat grade. The trail is a little grown in at sections, but still easy to follow. During the spring a great amount of wildflowers line the trail. After 1.6 miles of easy hiking you will cross a small stream and you'll be on the road mentioned above. The road immediately climbs from here along a dirt/rock footing. The going is very moderate over some sections with switchbacks to cut down on erosion. The closer you get to the summit, however, the steeper it gets and you'll encounter more rock slabs. Be very careful on the rock slabs because loose stones on slabs are a recipe for a bad slip. The road will bring you to just below the summit where a short trail comes in and finishes it off.

Approx. distance from trailhead: 3 miles
Approx. time: 4 to 6 hours RT
Approx. loop distance from trailhead: 5.5 miles

#67
Wakely Mountain
Elevation 3760'
Map #17

This 1500' climb to the top of one of the more popular fire tower summits is short and sweet; and steep. The summit is the home of the Adirondacks tallest fire tower at 80 plus feet high. When climbing this tower on a windy day you may find yourself swaying in the breeze. In fact, even if it isn't windy on the ground, it's still likely to be breezy on the tower.

This peak has open access during periods of no snow. But during periods where snow covers the ground the road is only maintained up to a certain point. So, if you want to climb Wakley in the winter prepare for an extra long walk into the trailhead. The possibilities of skiing in is also a good plan, but beware of snowmobiles, they pretty much own this section of road in the winter. However, a nice snowmobile owner may offer a ride to the trailhead if they felt so inclined.

*Via the Observatory Trail
*Trail
*Blue route
To find the trailhead follow the Cedar River Road located in Indian Lake. Go 12 miles from Rte 28/30. If you reach the Cedar River Gate you've gone about a half mile to far. Along the road there is a sign that reads "Wakely Mountain Observatory". This is the start of the logging road. There is a parking area just off the road for people to leave their car if they need to continue on foot. The logging road past this point is not really accessible at this time. Even with a lot of clearance and a 4-wheel drive vehicle; downed trees and flooding by beavers has made further access by motor vehicle impossible. There was also talk that the logging

116

road will be gated by the NYSDEC in the future; so make a mental note of that.

The old woods road is very flat all the way into where it stops along a brook. It starts out first passing a beaver dam on the left, which during wet weather is overflowing. There are many small brooks that you will need to cross, but nothing more than that for this section of the road which is roughly 1 mile long. Here there is a small wooden bridge to cross over a pretty little brook. Continue on the road, which is more like a path now, for around 0.75 miles, where a trail comes in on the right. If you continue straight for about 100 yards you will come to a small wet land are. I call this "Wakely Marsh". It's a beautiful spot, well worth a short look and a few snapshots; in the fall when the leaves are changing color it can be a most wonderful place.

You will now follow the trail that came in on the right. The trail is now very steep; in fact you will climb over 1100' in the last 1.2 miles. The trail climbs continuously over rock slab, up steep banks, and at times under trees, to just below the summit where a short trail comes in on the right. The trail to the right is only a hundred feet long, and leads to an old helicopter pad, now in disrepair. This was once used to supply the observers' cabin with the needed products. Just beyond are the summit and its tower. Not much for views can be had from the ground floor, but 360 degree views can be had from the cab of the tower. To the right is the old observers cabin, and to the right of that is the old outhouse. Snowy, Panther, Buell Mountains can be seen to the E, Blue Mountain a little more to the N, and Cellar Mountain to the S.

Distance from the parking area: 3 miles
Time from the parking area: 4 to 5 hours RT

Wakley Mountain fire tower in the clouds

#68
Henderson Mountain
Elevation 3752'
Map #18

You'll recognize the name Henderson from the popular lake newly acquired by New York State. What a lot of people don't know is it's also a mountain located directly W of the lake. You can find it snuggled up right behind the Bradley Pond Lean-to. Its slopes are the ones that drain the brook that campers so often use for their water supply when staying in the area. Now that you know, go climb it.

*Via Bradley Pond Lean-to
*Trail/Bushwhack
*Blue Route

Even though this route starts along a trail for most of the distance you will still have to bushwhack to the summit. You will want to start your hike at the trailhead that goes to both Duck Hole and the Santanoni's, in Tahawus.

The trail starts along a road which is privately owned-with easements for hikers. Please respect the land owners so we can keep on having use of this right of way. The trail leaves the road on the right after about 1.75 miles. Entering the woods you will soon find yourself crossing a small steam, Santanoni Brook, which is 2.25 miles from the car. The trail now climbs steadily but moderately up into the valley that splits the Santanoni Range and Henderson Mountain. Along the trail, you'll climb along the banks of Santanoni Brook and take in some of the great little cascading waterfalls. You will come to a height of land at about 3.8 miles and descend slightly to a very wet area. From here to the lean-to, it's wet, often with knee deep mud. Care is needed to trek from here. Even with the areas heavy use, the trail never seams to dry up completely. We often laugh that the mud goes from knee deep to only ankle deep.

At a little over 4 miles you will come to the shore of a marshy area; the beaver damn at the end of it is the path for the Santanoni's-you will need to continue on for 0.25 mile to the lean-to.

Once at the lean-to look for the brook that run past and through the trail, this will be your route. At first you will find it hard to follow to closely because of dead fall that crosses it and the thickness of the surrounding trees-it will get better. Keep the brook within ear shot and you will be fine. The summit is less than 0.5 miles from the lean-to; doesn't sound like much, does it? But plan on an hour to the summit. After about a quarter mile the woods open up and you will be able to spy a view or two of the Santanoni Range. The trees are much smaller and not quite as close together, the ground is covered in duff that is very soft under foot. Looking ahead you think you can see what looks like the summit ridge, but in fact is just a rise before the small knob of Henderson. From this rise you can see the summit only a couple hundred feet away. The summit boasts little for views, but is very peaceful, considering of course it's not bug season. We were there during peak bug season and our stay on the summit consisted of a handful of trail mix and couple bites of PB&J. Heck we even forgot to take pictures the black flies were so thick.

Again, your experience from the lean-to may differ. A friend of mine took a non-bushwhacking but experienced hiker, on a different day. His guest felt that the going was so tough, he swore off bushwhacking again. We descended down the SW ridge, which is described below.

Approx. distance from trailhead: 4.75 mile
Approx. time needed: 7 to 9 hours RT

Henderson Mountain from the Santanoni Trail

*Via the SW Ridge
*Trail/Bushwhack
*Green Route

Start from the same point as the above route and follow the trail to the height of land, this will start you close to the ridgeline you want. The summit is a mere 0.9 miles and 800' in elevation away in a straight line. Unfortunately, as you know there's no straight line when bushwhacking. Plan a little over an hour for this one.

The travel along the ridge isn't too bad. Occasionally a little thick in spots but nothing very steep. The terrain is moderate and very soft, the trees almost seem different on this side-probably just my imagination. At around 0.4 miles you will top a small rise with some miner views, a little bit of exploring might find you a decent one. Unfortunately we didn't have any extra time that day for any additional exploring. The climb is still very steady but on an ever so slightly steeper grade than in the beginning. The summit ridge is upon you after only another 0.3 miles atop a small lower bump. The true summit is just over 0.1 miles away, and a mere 40' higher.

Approx. distance from trailhead: 4.5 miles
Approx. time: 6 to 7 hours RT

Henderson Lake as seen from the Duck Hole Trail

122

#69
Lewey Mountain
Elevation 3742'
Map #19

Well what can I say about Lewey? It has a lake named after it as well as a state campsite both of which are wonderful. It has two prominent ridges that form a horseshoe which on a map looks pretty impressive. Actually it's pretty nice along the ridges too. But again don't take my word for, check it out for yourself-I recommend hiking the entire horseshoe ridge.

*Via the Sucker Brook Trail and the Southern Ridge
*Trail/Bushwhack
*Red and Blue Routes

The trail starts out flat and follows a lightly used path to an intersection with a dirt road that leads back to the campground. Follow here to the right and then bear left at the next intersection by the trail register. The trail descends slightly to a wet area that needs to be maneuvered. Once across here this very lightly used trail is a pleasure to walk on. Although most of the time it is easy to follow, there are a few small sections that are overgrown and the trail disappears in its cover. There are also a few sharp turns in the trail and small brook crossings that can be missed, so a little care and a sharp eye might be needed. You will need to follow the Sucker Brook Trail for around 3.25 miles finding yourself climbing very steadily to a small hogback. The trail will make a sharp turn south. This is where you depart, heading just west of north until you come across the valley between Lewey and the hogback. The ridge is directly N of you now.

We used this ridge as a descent route because we wanted to check out the smaller summit of Lewey, which ended up being thicker than the

123

actual top. If you keep your eyes pealed along this route, you could have the chance to see a moose-limited but it's possible. This ridge isn't extremely steep but steady all the way to the lower summit, which can easily be skirted to the SE. We found the woods from the trail to the summit very open a usual occurrence for the Adirondack 100 Highest peaks found in the Indian Lake area.

From Lewey's sub-peak, it is only 0.25 miles to the summit. The top is obstructed by trees, but unlike some of the others, you can see light through these. Either this route or the other one mentioned below would make a great descent route, but I will describe them as if you are climbing.

Approx. distance from trailhead: 4 miles
Approx. time: 6 to 6.5 hours

*Via the Sucker Brook Trail and the SE Ridge
*Trail/Bushwhack
*Red and Green Routes

The route starts at the same place as the above description but you will only follow the trail for 2.4 miles. The only real distinction along the trail is when you are at a small height of land: the trail then descends moderately, if you start going down hill, retrace your steps to that height of land. The ridge starts out very wide, but after 0.25 miles it narrows. The woods are very open up to this point. But, as with all narrow ridges, there's only so much room for everything to spread out and grow. Don't get me wrong it's not overly thick by any means, but it will get tighter as the ridge narrows and you notice a difference in the landscape. There will be a few small views through the trees. Snowy Mountain is prominent, and in autumn and winter be sure to pack your camera for the best pictures. The ridge remains narrow for about 0.5 miles before it widens as you approach the summit. This is a very nice hike, and quite enjoyable, providing open woods, small scrambles over steep sections, and fresh air-the lack of a summit view can't take that away.

Approx. distance from parking: 3.5 miles
Approx. time needed: 5 to 6 hours

Ferns and rocks along Lewey Mountain route

#70
Sawtooth #3
Elevation 3700'
Map #20

While there are those who like to approach from the N, it seems that a majority approach from Duck Hole. The other approach is from Lake Placid via the Northville Placid Trail. I have not approached this peak via the NPT Trail, so the information from this direction is a compilation of others who've done it that way.

*Via Northville Placid Trail
*Trail/Bushwhack
*Green Route

The longest section to bag this peak is the hike along the Northville Placid Trail. Your day will start at the trailhead on Averyville Road, with a 8.8 mile trail walk ahead of you-that's just to the start of this bushwhack route.

Having hiked this section of trail a couple times now, I know to expect wet sections, beautiful sections, and long boring sections with very little change in elevation. The trail basically follows the Chubb River all the way from Averyville Road to its head waters. At 6.5 miles you will come to Wanika Falls. With a few more easy ups and downs you will find yourself at Moose Pond and the amazing views of the Sawtooth Range that tower above it. From here it's about 0.4 miles to the start of the bushwhack. Stay along the trail until you have traveled around the small knob that sits just south of Moose Pond.

Here you will leave the trail and cross Moose Creek. Depending on where you hit the brook, or the time of year you may have to wade to start your rugged bushwhack of 1.5 miles to the summit of Sawtooth #3. As soon as you cross the brook, it is flat for a short stretch before the steady steep climb kicks in. You will enter a small ravine after 0.6 miles that will guide you between two small bumps in the shoulder. The woods still aren't over powering, however you will find they begin to close in the closer you get to the summit. At 0.9 miles into the bushwhack the terrain gets much steeper; in fact you will climb 1000' in the next 0.65 miles to the summit. Depending on how direct your route from here, you may encounter a few small cliffs which will slow progress down to a near halt at times.

Views from the summit are little; the best ones are found along the way as you look back. This route is very long but makes for a very nice overnight at Wanika Falls, combined with a short bushwhack up Three Peaks to get warmed up…but that's another story.

Approx. distance from Averyville Rd: 10.25 miles
Approx. time: 12 to 14 hours RT from Averyville Rd
                6 to 6.5 hours RT from camp at Wanika Falls

*Via Duck Hole
*Trail/Bushwhack
*Blue route
This route is only slightly shorter than the above but the bushwhack is a hair longer. As I mentioned, I believe this is the preferred route. You should again prepare for a long day in the woods, and a pace of about 0.5 miles an hour once you leave the trail.

Starting from Upper Works you will find yourself on a gravel road that leads to the southern approaches of a number of the High Peaks. The road soon crosses an inlet to the Hudson River before coming to an intersection. The right intersection leads to Calamity Pond and Flowed Lands where High Peaks like Colden, Cliff, Marshall, and many others

Climbing a waterfall in route to Sawtooth #3

can be climbed. Continue left still along an older section not as well maintained as the other trail. The trail will begin to climb through some wet and muddy sections, you will need to step carefully through some of these and use the corduroy that has been laid out to keep your feet dry. The trail will then descend moderately for around 0.5 miles before flattening out at another intersection. Straight leads into Indian Pass, and left drops down to a bridge, go left.

The trail starts by following the N shore of Henderson Lake before breaking away at the sight of a new lean-to. From here the trail just rolls along, with small ups and downs. The terrain is quite nice, lightly used, soft under foot. There are small rocky sections to walk through but nothing that will slow you down much. The continuous, year round muddy sections you will encounter are another story. There is a brook crossing near Lower Preston Ponds that can be quite tricky, but if you go up stream a little ways you might be able to find a tree over the inlet that you can catwalk; or a little further up there is a small beaver flow you can jump. But that could all change over time, that's part of the fun of exploring. After a decent climb and descent you will find yourself at the former home of a bridge that once spanned Roaring Brook. You will now have to rock hop it to the other side. During high water this will be impossible to rock hop; wading will be your only choice. So carry a towel just in case the water has submerged the rocks. I recommend the use of a trekking pole for this crossing, as balance is the key.

Once across the brook you will see the trail goes in two directions. Left goes to the Duck Hole Lean-to and the Ward Brook region. Right goes in the direction you want. You will follow here for 0.9 miles. This short section is part of the Northville Placid Trail and is relatively flat. But what's relative when hiking? If carrying an altimeter or GPS, you will begin your bushwhack at 2215' in elevation. Looking to your left you will see that there is a low valley between small peaks. The valley is roughly 70 feet higher than where you are standing. Climb to the top of that valley which is 0.15 miles away. Directly through the valley there is a very small bump that I recommend you climb. On the way in we skirted it to the SW and found ourselves in some really thick evergreens. On

129

the way in we skirted it to the SW and found ourselves in some really thick evergreens. On the way out we climbed over it in hopes to avoid that and it did. You will not need to go over the exact top, but climb over the shoulder and keep the top on your right. Once over the shoulder and down the other side you will be at the shore of Moose Creek. This band of water is about 25' across with no rocks to hop-at least in this area. We took off our socks and boots and waded across. The rocks are a little sharp under foot but that's better than wet feet all day. Oh, as a small suggestion-don't carry your boots in your hands just in case you need to catch yourself if you slip-your boots will still get wet. Strap them to your pack or sling them over your shoulder.

On the other side of the brook you'll find the bushwhack you've eagerly been waiting for. Right off there is a small cliff to skirt to the left, the woods are a little thick, but manageable. This will put you in a small grassy valley with steeps slopes in front. At this point you need to go over this rise and back down the other side to a small stream crossing. Cross over and start your climb of Sawtooth #3. Don't go too far to the right or you'll find yourself in patches of thicker fir trees. Keep pushing up and to the left until you encounter a stream. Between 2400' and 2500' along the brook there is a nice little waterfall of about 50'. You can climb it rather easily on the left, and follow it along its slabs for quite a while. The brook takes you in the right direction and eventually dies out. At this point however the woods are very open and easy to navigate. Just go from grassy section to grassy section, and lightly wooded to lightly wooded sections, and before you know it you will be in an open black spruce forest with the summit getting closer and closer. As mentioned earlier the summit offers little in the way of views, but small ones can be had with a little bit of exploring. The best views will be those from the descent along the steep slopes that got you here. Your satisfaction will be with a bushwhack well done. Take a break and enjoy it, as you've got a long way back to the car.

Approx. distance from Upper Works: 9 miles
Approx. time: 12 to 14 hours RT from the Upper Works

Open Woods on Sawtooth #3

#71
Wallface Mountain
Elevation 3700'
Map #1

Wallface Mountain is home of peregrine falcons and rock climbers alike. The only difference is falcons live there and the climbers wish they could. The face of this mountain can be seen clearly from most of the ridge in the MacIntyre Range, and is put into perspective with AWE when viewed from Summit Rock by passing hikers. With the route following the outlet to Wallface Ponds you will climb near some of the ledges that inspire so many to keep both feet on the ground.

*Via Wallface Pond Outlet
*Trail/Bushwhack
*Black Route

It was 87 degrees with 90% humidity. That's a day you don't want to get out of bed, much less climb a High Peak. I must have been daydreaming when that rule got talked about, because the last time I hiked this route, we were fighting and sweating our way up Wallface.

The ride over to the Upper Works was filled with coffee, muffins as well as hopes for a great climb. Boy, were we going to be surprised. This was my second trip up Wallface, but my last was a good eight years ago and my memories were getting a little foggy.

As we did, you'll depart from the trailhead at Upper Works/Tahawus. The trail is rather straightforward; first passing the trail to Flowed Lands on the right, then the trail to Duck Hole on the left. The only issue we had was the lack of a bridge over Indian Pass Brook that we needed to cross. This crossing is roughly 2 miles from the trailhead. Unfortunately,

132

we were here after a month-long pounding of rain and the brook was showing the obvious signs. We went down stream, no luck. We went upstream, then further upstream, then eventually further upstream and finally our only hope was to rock hop one section. With the help of a couple old tree limbs lying on the ground I managed to get across without a obtaining a drop of water. Once across, I watched for Alan. He is a close friend and Wallface was going to be his 97th peak. Looking slightly down stream from me I see him putting on garbage bags over his boots to wade across, holding the draw strings. To this day I kick myself for not taking a picture. But while thinking that's a great idea. I now have a set in my pack.

Once across the brook we bushwhacked our way back to the trail, after a 2.5 miles hike we quickly found ourselves at the Wallface lean-to. After a short break we turned on the GPS and headed off to the Wallface Pond Outlet stream which is only 0.4 miles from the lean-to. If you follow our tracks, you'll bushwhack/rock hop to a beautiful vly located only 0.6 miles up the brook. The vly is the turning point in the route to the summit of Wallface. Leaving the brook before that point is kind of senseless, as you'll just end up fighting more cliffs along that side of the mountain. Besides, the vly is something you don't want to miss, especially during the fall foliage season.

You know how I mentioned rock hop before? Well that was the plan, unfortunately the previous bout of rain made the rocks wet, slippery and most of the time, underwater (During times of normal water level this brook can be traveled rather easily). As you should, we adapted to the situation and hiked along the right side of the brook, returning to it only to take in a waterfall or two. There is one gorgeous waterfall, which cascades into a deep pool. It's located roughly 0.25 miles from the trail. The terrain starts to get much steeper now, but is still rather open, which was very pleasing for us. Unfortunately, we found ourselves a little too high and far from the brook, and needed to get back to it in order to see the "light" at the end. What I mean by the "light" is the point where the brook exits the vly. There is a small water fall just feet before this, and you will be standing below the waterfall and all you can see is a window

The vly on the Wallface Pond Outlet

of light above the waterfall and a wide open space. It really is quite a sight. When you arrive at the vly, take the time for a long break so you can take in its gem like quality. Sunny, my four-legged hiking partner took a dip to cool off. With the heat and bugs, we found ourselves really behind on time, as far as where we thought we would be by noon. The vly is where the real work begins, and you'll leave the comfort zone of the brook and hit the upper woods.

The forest here is a mess along the entire right shore of the vly. Luckily, you won't have to endure it too much longer. The vly has a narrow ring of thick trees around it, mixing nicely with a coating of blow down. Once past, the woods opened up nicely. In fact we referred to these woods as fernwhacking. These conditions will get you through this section in good time to start a steep, relentless climb. In the valley between the vly and Wallface is a rocky slope, the rocks are moss-covered, and mixed in with new growth, scrubs, and trees, making for a rather difficult walk.

We were now off the rocks and on an extremely steep slope of unstable duff that exited us at the base of one of Wallface's cliff bands. We hit this section about 0.3 miles from the vly. This was actually a really easy fix. The band went uphill, with a natural walkway right along its base. About 100 yards up along the cliffs was a small mossy slope that we climbed to get us to the top of this band. It was a fitness challenge of strength and endurance. Being practically a vertical climb, the ground had a hard time holding our weight, and the second person up had it even worse. Normally we wouldn't take such a steep slope for fear of a sudden stop, but we weren't sure if we would have another opportunity right away. The top of the cliffs brought us some rather scratchy trees and more steep slopes. We did manage to find a small runoff that made for a decent open route a few hundred more vertical feet. But like all things good, they don't usually last. Now it really was getting thick, a lot of pushing and pulling among the trees and us with a few grunts, a lot of cursing, and talking to ourselves. Alan calling out for me to hold up, but he's only 20 feet behind, and can't see me it's so thick. Then, all of a sudden, we were on a small bump. This bump is located almost directly W of Wallface, 0.5 miles from the vly.

Well, it's not exactly where we wanted to be, but the good news is that we're out of the thick stuff and off the cliffs. The bad news was that the summit was over to our left, on the other side of a massive blow down field. I was now concerned about time, as we were only 0.3 miles away from the summit, but with the heat, humidity and terrain, it could take over an hour. We lucked out though, as the blow down was only on one side of the ridge. We dropped below the ridge just enough to skirt the damage and the woods never really got thick again, just a little tight in spots, with a couple trees lying across the route, but never really thick.

We were now on the wooded summit of Wallface. When I was up there the first time, the summit was heavily wooded on all sides. Now, one entire side has been leveled by hard, wet winters and severe winds. But now there's a view to look at. Lost Pond Peak, sections of the Seward's, and the Sawtooth Range were all in view right from the large rock that marks the top. While sitting on top in the intense heat, I happened to notice an area that was quite open through the trees that led off in the other direction toward the cliffs. So, I grabbed my camera and checked it out. This really lightly use herd trail led to the top of a small cliff, opening up views of the entire MacIntyre Range, and most of Tahawus, Lake Henderson, and Santanoni's. In my opinion and that of Alan's, this is the best view of the trailless lower 54.

We decided to take the short bushwhack out, by continuing along the ridge and meeting up with the Indian Pass Trail on the Lake Placid side. Please see that route below as an alternative ascent route.

Approx. distance from Upper Works: 4.5 miles
Approx. time: 8 to 10 hours RT

*Via Indian Pass from the North
*Trail/Bushwhack
*Green Route
This is possibly the easiest route to the summit of Wallface-more trail hiking, less bushwhacking, and clearer woods to travel through. I usually use this as a descent route but it ends up being a preferred ascent route as well. But don't let me be the sole judge of that, you try both and see what you think. This route starts from the Adirondack Loj Trailhead parking and follows the Indian Pass Trail to the start of the bushwhack.

Starting from the Loj make sure to return to the gate and cross the road, the trail is on the other side. The start of the trail is quite busy-passing other junctions, a nature center, and a few benches as part of a naturetrail. I've also found this trail to be very sporadic as far as condition. One day it's dry as a bone and the next it's a muddy wallow. Either way it makes for a nice hike. Along the trail you'll pass by both ends of the Rocky Falls Loop, which I highly recommend you check out some time. You will also wander by the Scott Clearing Lean-to, which is in fact nowhere near Scott Clearing.

You will come to Scott Clearing after the lean-to and it's very obvious when you're there. It's a beautiful place, especially in mid spring and fall. You will notice at the far end lies Wallface, your goal. There is a high water route just before Scott Clearing that follows the top of the ridge above, some times of the year this is the only way through to the areas on the other side. During low water, I recommend walking through the clearing.

Once through the clearing there is a short hike to another trail intersection, which is Cold Brook Pass or also known as Iroquois Pass. Keep on the Indian Pass Trail for a little longer until you cross Indian Pass Brook for the last time and it makes a sharp flowing turn into the woods to your right. The brook is now passing into a col to the NW between Wallface and another unnamed bump. This will be the start of your bushwhack.

The woods are a little thick here at first but nothing really outrageous. The woods will open up a little as you go. You will then encounter a couple small cliffs. These cliffs are easily skirted either to the right or left, and in spots could be scrambled to the top. Above the cliffs, nice open woods-these conditions will last for a long time. Something to keep in mind on this route up; don't stray to far right, that's where the blow down is. By blow down I mean total devastation, the entire side of the mountain was leveled by harsh winters and heavy winds. Going to far to the left can bring you out to the sheer cliffs that Wallface is so famous for. So, keep it on the straight and narrow and the woods will stay friendly.

As the ridge starts to mellow out and become less steep, you can wander carefully over toward the cliffs and take in the numerous views that dot this route. Be very careful near the ledges, it can be very unstable and slippery. In spring you will also have a good chance of seeing peregrine falcons flying about, who nest on the cliffs. The summit is approached through tight black spruce, on a hard pack summit floor. Small herd paths from past climbers mark several different approaches along the last 0.2 miles. The summit is a boulder just on the edge of the blow down field. Lost Pond Peak, sections of the Sewards and the Sawtooths are all in view right from the large rock that marks the top. There is a really light herd trail on the cliff side that leads to the top of a small cliff, opening up views of the entire MacIntyre Range, and most of Tahawus, Lake Henderson, and Santanoni's. In my opinion the best view from a trailless lower 54.

Return via this ascent route, or if a second car is spotted at Upper Works, use the other route for Wallface to make for an extra long and rewarding adventure.

Approx. distance from Loj: 5.5 miles
Approx. time: 7 to 8 hours RT

The MacIntyre Range from Wallface Mountain

Wallface Mountain as seen from Indian Pass

<u>#72</u>
<u>Hurricane Mountain</u>
<u>Elevation 3694'</u>
<u>Map #21</u>

If Hurricane isn't the most climbed summit of "The Other 54" it has to be close. If you've never climbed it, I am sure you've at least seen it. No one can miss the fire tower that stands on its summit, as if to guard-but that may be short lived. After being built so long ago, it is on the DEC's death row. Some believe for safety reasons and for others as it's a "non-conforming structure" in a wilderness area. These routes have been written to death so I'm going to just do a quick overview of what to expect along the three used trails to Hurricane's 360 degree views.

*Via Rte. 9N
*Trail
*Green Route

The trail starts out right away at a steep climb for 0.3 miles. Quite eroded in spots but very dry. It then flattens out to a nice footpath, passing through open woods, over corduroy, through mud, and over passing brooks. The trail passes by a marsh area, with a floating cat walk. This is an excellent spot for birding. The trail then passes through a very muddy section close to a marsh, with not much for dry footing.

The trail now starts to climb steadily for a short bit to another flat section, now in an open hardwood forest. After this short flat area the trail starts a long steady and at times steep climb to the intersection with the trail from Crow Clearing. Along this section be prepared for large rocks, slabs, and wet footing.

In the intersection there is a sign pointing you right. You will climb along the summit rocks for 0.2 miles to the summit cone and its mass expanse of open views. The views are wide open. They range from the surrounding High Peaks to the Crows and Nun-da-ga-o Ridge to Weston Mountain. Mount Mansfield and Camels Hump in Vermont are in view to the E. The fire tower which is deemed unsafe to climb probably is. The DEC has removed the two lower sections of the staircase and two of the platforms. The fire tower cab is still in decent shape, but all glass windows have been removed.

Distance from Rte 9N: 2.6 miles
Time needed: 3.5 hours RT

A view from Hurricane Mountain

*Via Crow Clearing
*Trail
*Red Route

Crow Clearing can be found just outside the Village of Keene along a dirt road, which is unmaintained in the winter and quite rough in the summer. Follow Hurricane Road out of Keene to O'Toole Road, Crow Clearing Road is a right off that road. From Crow Clearing the trail heads SE crossing a bridge over a branch of Gulf Brook. The route is very level for 1.1 miles to Gulf Brook Lean-to, a very nice spot to spend a quiet night. The trail crosses the brook next to the lean-to and begins a very gradual ascent crossing a brook many times. It then climbs a little steeper to the junction with the Rte 9N trail at 2.8 miles. From here it is the same 0.2 mile hike to the summit rocks described above.

Distance from Crow Clearing: 3 miles
Time needed: 3.5 to 4 hours RT

*Via Hurricane Road from the East
*Trail
*Blue Route

This is the steepest approach of all three, but a very interesting one, and my favorite. From the looks of the trail this one is used the least of all three, making it the most wild. At just under 3 miles up Hurricane Road in Elizabethtown there is a small parking area on the right. If you come to a gate you have gone to far, retrace your steps. The parking area has enough room for 4-5 cars, depending of course on the size of the cars. The end of the road is 1.25 miles, and the old site of the observer's cabin, looking around you can find bits and pieces of old junk that were tossed about. From this point the trail drops slightly to a brook crossing before a steep climb begins. The trail is a steady climb with little opportunity for a break and doesn't let up until you reach the open rocks 0.1 miles from the actual summit. During a wet spree this trail tends to be very wet, with what could be called a stream running right down the center of it.

Distance from gate: 2.7 miles
Time needed: 3 hours RT

Hurricane Mountain in winter from the Hurricane Road approach

#73
Hoffman Mountain
Elevation 3693'
Map #22

Hoffman mountain has so many approaches that are feasible, it's simply a matter of which once appeals to you the most. However, with a second car this also opens up a few loop opportunities. When preparing yourself for this peak, you should ready yourself for periods of very thick woods and sections of blowdown, no matter which side of the peak you decide to take.

*Via the South Ridge
*Trail/Bushwhack
*Blue Route

This route starts off from the Hoffman Road with comes out of Schroon Lake. Follow Hoffman Road for a little over 2 miles, you will first cross over I-87; the trail will be on the right. It's unmarked by any trail sign, but there is a place to park for a few cars. You'll see a trail disk on a tree, but the trail is very obvious. The trail will lead you along an old road through an old stand forest. The going is very flat and muddy in spots, but very fast. After about 10 minutes your first landmark will be a bridge that crosses an inlet to a marsh on your left. This is a very picturesque area. The trail from here continues to be very moderate on a steady course just W of N. After around 1.3 miles you will descend slightly to a low area near Big Pond. After another 0.3 miles you will be directly N of Big Pond and at the base of the south ridge to Hoffman. Starting the bushwhack here; you'll be traveling N, steadily upward, to the narrow ridge and eventually to the summit 3.5 miles away.

This route starts as a steep climb to the ridge and continues through open woods. Be sure to keep to the E side of the ridge for a few reasons. It's more open over there, this is where the views are, and the herd path may disappear here and there into downed brush. After about 0.75 miles, the herd path will become apparent, and will lead you to a large array of views to the E, NE and SE. The first view point will blow your mind; it's atop a grassy area inhabited by tall hardwoods and ferns. North Pond can be seen below as well as Jones Hill to the E. From here, continue along the herd path through more open woods. If you ever loose the trail, which I assure you it will happen at times, return to the E edge of the ridge and pick it up again. If you find yourself in woods that are a little thicker than expected, you're too far to the W of the ridge and you should return toward the E side, without descending onto the steep slopes of the ridge.

After about 1.1 miles you will come to a very steep grassy slope and the herd path will zig-zag up the section to a super view to the S. The path will come and go, but seems to reappear when you need it the most. Again the woods are generally pretty open up to the last 0.75 miles; expect more blowdown than you previously experienced. The ridge doglegs slightly to the NE, and this is where the woods start to close in a bit. The herd path now is very easy to follow and guides you through the thicker woods and over a couple small steep sections all the way to the top. The summit is marked with a small rock cairn, and is fully wooded. There are some views to the N and NW and the Dix Range stand tall to the N. Blue Ridge can be slightly seen through the trees.

Approx. distance from parking: 5.25 miles
Approx. time: 9 to 9.5 hours RT

*Via Blue Ridge
*Bushwhack
*Green Route

Leaving the summit of Blue Ridge is a real challenge as was getting there. The trees are very close together and sharp, making for a slightly painful climb. The descent to the col between Blue Ridge and Hoffman is a chore. The woods are old and very unstable, and in spots, very scratchy with dead spruce branches. Don't go too far to the E or W it's like nothing you've ever seen. In fact you can't see a thing. Your hiking

Hoffman Mountains open woods along the South Ridge

partner can be 10 feet in front of you, and if it weren't for the swearing you probably wouldn't even know they were there. The ground you know is under you, at least most of the time-but you can't even see where you're stepping.

Once in the col, you're about half way there, but woods are no less forgiving from here to the summit of Hoffman. In fact, the going might even be a little thicker. You will find yourself spreading the trees apart to step in between them, and surprise, here's another downed tree to step over while you're doing it. Don't wander too far to the W. We did and found a couple sections of nasty blowdown to skirt. Just below the summit of Hoffman you'll come to a nice lookout back toward Blue Ridge. The best views are in fact along that nasty 0.2 miles of never ending thick you just came through. The trees are dense but they're short and an occasional piece of downfall mixed in makes for a nice personal soapbox to stand on. That's about all you'll find in ways of views along this short section, so drink it up.

Approx. distance between the two summits: 1.1 miles
Approx. time: 1.5 to 2 hours; one way

*Via Hoffman Notch
*Trail/Bushwhack
*Black Route

The Hoffman Notch Trailhead can be found along the Blue Ridge Road that connects North Hudson to Newcomb. This trail traverses a gorgeous mountain pass, open fields and brooks that have been inhabited for generations by beaver.

At the start, the trail will drop slightly to the shore of the brook and soon crosses two footbridges that put you into an open field of green. Soon after, you will come to a powerline just before entering the pass. About 0.3 miles from the powerline, the trail will start to climb into Hoffman Notch and becomes very narrow in spots, with cliffs and steep slopes from Washburn Ridge and Hornet Cobbles. Boulders litter the notch,

147

some as big as large vehicles. The brook meanders down over numerous small cascades. The approach is in an absolutely gorgeous area, one that should be visited even if climbing a peak isn't on the agenda.

At 3.5 miles you will reach the shores of Big Marsh. It's worth visiting, but it's about 0.25 miles too far if your going to climb the peak. Keep this in mind as you are going in. The actual start of this route begins with the marsh to your right and a small pond to your left. There is a high ground between the two; this will keep you out of the really wet areas. The woods are pretty thick as you will be able to tell from the trees lining the trail on the way in. In fact the terrain really remains pretty thick for most of this route, and blowdown will also slow your progress to the summit. Once through the valley of the two bodies of water you will continue to climb, bearing east, and cross a brook that feeds the pond mentioned above. At this spot cross and enter the draw of another drainage that flows from Hoffman. The slopes here are equally as thick as below, and much steeper. You may need to climb along the slopes of the draw to avoid small areas of blowdown. This route will deliver you just to the S of the summit of Hoffman. From here to the summit, it will feel like a walk in the park compared to what you just went through.

Approx. distance from trailhead: 6.2 miles
Approx time: 9 to 10 hours RT

*Via the East and Peaked Hills
*Trail/Bushwhack
*Red Route

To find the beginning of this route, follow these directions. Get off exit 28 of I-87 (Adirondack Northway). Turn left at the four-way stop and head north on Rte 9. You will shortly come to the Schroon River Bridge, don't cross it. Instead, you should take the dirt road before it on the left. The road will follow the west bank of the river and looks as though it should be posted-but isn't (that could change over time). Continue to follow it until you come to a transmission line and a small grassy pull off-park here. Follow the transmission line S to a stream that leads under I-87. There is a culvert here for deer crossings that you can use to access the other side of the interstate.

Follow the stream W until it turns N and away from Peaked Hills. This is about 0.5 miles from the culvert. Once you leave the brook you will need to make a bearing between the two eastern Peaked Hills. You'll climb about 900' in the next mile to just descend to the col between it and the western Peaked Hill. Be sure to stay south of this hill to avoid having to reclimb too much. Once around this obstacle and on the main mass of Hoffman, the terrain will turn from an open hardwood forest to a thicker spruce stand. As you proceed upward to within 0.5 miles of the summit, you will be maneuvering around small cliff bands and much thicker spruce. This is not by any means the worst climb out there, but the last mile will take about as long as the whole rest of the trip.

Approx. distance from parking: 3.75 miles
Approx time: 8 to 9 hours RT

A nice section on Hoffman Mountain

Sunny on the summit of Hoffman Mountain

#74
Cheney Cobble
Elevation 3683'
Map #10

If possible, Cheney Cobble is a peak that should be combined with North River Mountain, because the approach to this peak goes over the shoulder of North River Mountain-hence saving you climbing in the long run. So plan for a really long day in the middle of nowhere and bag them both.

*Via the North
*Bushwhack
*Red Route
I can't suggest strongly-enough that you obtain permission or join the East River Club before even thinking about the following these routes.

This route starts almost directly N along a branch of Dudley Brook. Located at the end of the private access road, it's guarded by the East River Club and many miles of approach. At this point there is a small parking area for a half dozen cars-this is where we parked. We continued along the deteriorating jeep road on foot for a ways, to the site of an even older woods road. Now overgrown from years of non-use, nature is healing itself. However, even being healed it's easy to follow and provides a wonderful path to follow up to within 0.75 miles of the summit of Cheney Cobble.

Within five minutes the road begins to climb away from the brook and up the moderately steep slopes of North River Mountains. The road lasts for around 0.5 miles and should take about 30 minutes to complete. Of course there are the usual suspects; the brook crossings and the sporadic blowdown to overcome. All in all-it's a nice section of woods.

While following the road we found ourselves getting further and further from the brook. Then, once the road disappeared we continued going too far to the left. We found the woods over here to be extremely friendly, not like the nightmare we were told we would experience. We were warned of unforgiving blowdown, thick conifers, and walls of rock. I guess we missed it all going too far left. Someone was looking out for us. So, my recommendations would be to hang around the left side of the ridges that lead to Cheney Cobble. We did manage to see some cliffs around the summit crown, but, they were really manageable. The summit has some really great and unique views; views that can't be explained fully through words.

Approx. distance from private road: 3.25 miles
Approx. time: 8 to 10 hours RT
Approx. distance for loop over both peaks: 7 miles
Approx. time for loop: 10 to 12 hours

View from Cheney Cobble

*Via North River Mountain
*Bushwhack
*Blue Route
For details please see North River Mountain section in this guide (page 80).

Steep descent between Cheney Cobble and North River Mountain

#75
Calamity Mountain
Elevation 3620'
Map #23

Calamity sits in the shadows of the MacIntyre Range and overlooks the waters of Flowed Lands, but seldom gets the recognition of its bigger sisters. Maybe that's because there's no trail, or it's littered with blowdown, or, maybe it's because the views are lacking. Whatever the reason I'm going to tell you that this peak has an unseen potential; you'll see.

The last two routes below are the series of a loop that I had taken, the first of the two was my ascent route the later was my descent. I'll give you my ascent route as a warning to use my descent route for both directions.

*Via Southeast Slide
*Trail/Bushwhack
*Red Route

Slide climbing is becoming a very popular approach to many mountains, such as; Colden, Lower Wolf Jaw, Kilburn, Dix, and now Calamity. Just remember that slide climbing is a dangerous activity that requires climbers to use common sense and proper gear. This approach crosses private land leased by the East River Club-the trail you are using is an easement, leaving it would break that easement. Please get permission to approach the slide.

So, if you're ready to begin, get yourself to Tahawus and the trailhead for Adams and Allen. The trail starts off following a road to the banks of the Hudson River, where it turns hard right to a suspension bridge over the river. On the other side of the bridge you will find yourself back on

154

the road and hiking flat to the shore of Lake Jimmy. There is a long floating bridge over the lake. This bridge at times is in disrepair and quite often slippery. Use caution, a slip can end a hike real fast. The lake isn't really deep through here, but it only takes a few inches of water to soak through. The end of the bridge brings you back to the trail and at about 0.75 miles from the junction with the Adams Mountain Trail. Continue hard right along the trail to a gravel road.

Continue following this road until a footpath comes in. The footpath is very easy to recognize, and there will be a few of them. Then in just under 2 miles you will be at the shore of Lake Sally. There will be a few views across the lake. Shortly beyond that comes the Opalescent River, as you hike along the road that parallels it you will notice a few private cabins-please respect the owner's privacy. At about 3.4 miles from the parking lot you will cross the river and hike along its right side. After a few brook crossings the trail enters the old site of the Twin Brook Lean-to. This is the intersection with the Allen Mountain herd path; follow the trail to the left and cross Upper Twin Brook.

This trail is pretty moderate with light use. Being the long approach to Flowed Lands it gets little attention from hikers, and still has a somewhat decent amount of blowdown scattered throughout. The start of the bushwhack is approximately 5.8 miles from the parking area.

From the trail, descend down a blowdown filled bank to the shore of the Opalescent River, then find a place to cross. This could be one of the biggest challenges of the day. High waters could cause you to have to remove your boots and ford the river or find different means of crossing.

The slide isn't a single band of rock as the topo map might suggest, but rather a series of parallel bands. You will have to keep crossing through grown in areas to find the best possible open route, but this doesn't present a problem. The grade is moderate and the rock bare and dry until it gets closer to the top. Here the steepness combined with loose moss and lichen makes it somewhat treacherous, proper footing is essential. Although steep up to within 0.25 miles of the summit, the woods are never really thick, and don't require a lot of gymnastics to negotiate. The summit offers nothing for views, even in winter. But the unique views from the slide open up an entirely different world.

Use one of the following routes to complete a loop, and avoid descending the slide. A one car loop could be done, but you will need to walk the road from Upper Works back to the parking area, a distance of approximately 0.75 miles.

Approx. distance from Parking Lot: 6.75 Miles
Approx. time: 10 to 11 hours RT

*Via the West
*Trail/Bushwhack
*Blue Route
As I mentioned above, I don't recommend this route by any means, up or down. We left the trail about 0.2 miles from the foot bridge that crosses Calamity Brook. When we did it the woods had a very nice appearance at this point, so we jumped in and hoped for the best. We had no prior experience on this summit or word of mouth about the terrain. You're already one step ahead.

Soon after we entered the woods the trees started to come to life, slapping us around like rag dolls. It wasn't thick, just a lot of dead branches poking around. We then came to the next obstacle, a blowdown patch compliments of Hurricane Floyd. On our ascent we were forced to do a sick form of tight rope walking, using downed trees. This section took us about an hour to go 0.2 miles-no joke. What came next was the nicest thing about this section, a mini slide. The slide had some nice views but was very slippery, if you happen to find it be sure to tread lightly. The route from here to the flat section along the summit ridge was pretty thick, scratchy, and slowed us up a little. The ridge itself was very bearable, a little scratchy that's all. No views from the summit unfortunately. But its amazing how 0.9 mile bushwhack can take 3 hours. Use the following route as your route, you'll thank me later.

Approx. distance from Upper Works: 3.75 miles
Approx. time: 8 to 9 hours RT

Small slide on the northwest side of Calamity Mountain

*Via the North from Calamity Pond
*Trail/Bushwhack
*Green Route

This is the route you want to take to the summit of Calamity-hands
down. Hike the Calamity Brook Trail from Upper Works to the shore of
Calamity Pond and start your bushwhack there. The trail is very straight
forward, starting along a jeep road to Calamity Brook. A suspension
bridge crosses the brook and enters the woods to a foot trail. The trail
has a few wet spots along the way, and at about 1.8 miles it starts to
climb to Calamity Pond. Calamity Mountain becomes very apparent
to your right. At 3.5 miles is the jump off point for the bushwhack. The
woods look a little tight through here, but they aren't so bad once you
get inside and start hiking.

It's pretty cut and dry, semi-open woods, very little blow down, nice
lookouts along the way, a nice little climb to the top. Truth is it will take
you half the time to cover about the same distance and elevation as it
does from the W.The terrain isn't very steep over 80% of the distance
and the other 20% is all in how you approach it. There are steep
sections, but those sections usually open up the views from the top of
them, you could avoid them, but I wouldn't. There are some spectacular
views down into Flowed Lands through Avalanche Pass, with Colden to
the right and the MacIntyre's to the left.

Approx. distance from Upper Works: 4.75 miles
Approx. time: 7 to 8 hours RT

View along North route to Calamity Mountain

#76
Little Moose Mountain
Elevation 3620'
Map #24

Little Moose Mountain has a long approach along a trail rarely visited; it flows through the remote lands of West Canada Lakes, and the Moose River Plains. You will be visiting areas where moose roam and beaver flourish, where hawks soar and blue heron feast. You will fall in love with an area as precious as this.

*Via Butter Brook and Snowmobile Trail
*Trail/Bushwhack
*Blue Route

First stop by the ranger cabin at Wakely Dam and sign in as a visitor. This trail can be tricky to find. Begin by driving down the dirt road and start looking for camp site #24; it will be on the left. The camp is actually down a short dirt road, with a couple other small camps along it. Camp #24 is the last camp, right on Moose River; the trail is directly across the river. The bridge that used to cross it is long gone and you will need to wade it or wait for low water and cross on a few well placed rocks. The snowmobile trail that you will follow starts out very open and wide but the further you go the more it looks as though it will be over grown and difficult follow in a couple more years. The trail goes in and out of wet areas and finally comes to the crossing of Butter Brook at 2.4 miles. The crossing isn't as bad as it looks. Beavers have flooded the trail but also built you a bridge. Leave the trail on the right and walk to the flooded area. Cross a beaver dam where you can find one and you should be able to cross Butter Brook and be dry on the other side.

160

Crossing one of the beaver dams

Once across climb the small hill on the other side. Your next obstacle will now be to cross Moose River and that is a little tougher. Don't head right down to the river walk along the ridge above and you will find a small herd path, follow this for about 0.1 miles until you see a grassy area along the river. Look for another dam near here or prepare to wade across.

High elevation beaver pond

Once across the river, take a heading just E of S until you hit a very pleasant brook, which you will follow on and off. Don't feel you need to stay along this brook as the woods are very open. You will come to a rather steep section on the mountain which is just below a small beaver pond at 2785'. This pond is a very nice spot, one worth the trip in itself. Cross at the W end for the best view of the pond. There will be some small cliffs after the pond that will need to be avoided, but you can do so quite easily. Most of the remaining climb to the summit is through open woods. With 0.1 miles to go it closes in a little, but not bad.

The summit offers amazing views off one side on top of a small rocky ledge. This spot is just E of a mutually high point along the ridge which has no views. Either spot could be called the summit-both had equal elevation readouts. If you are a student of Adirondack history, look about. There is reportedly an original Colvin bolt somewhere up there. Take a picture for us if you locate it.

Approx. distance from camp #24: 4 miles
Approx. time: 7 to 10 hours RT

#77
Sunrise Mountain
Elevation 3614'
Map #25

 Sunrise Mountain is a gem, but to enjoy it you'll need to be a guest at the Elk Lake Lodge to use their trails. It's well worth it to spend the money. The rooms and cabins are wonderful and they have a large trail system on the property.

*Via Elk Lake's Private Trail
*Trail
*Red Route

This map shows the basic route of the trail, but it's very easy to follow, so a map is really just a safety precaution.

Follow the Dix Trail 0.2 miles to a four way intersection, labeled Clear Pond Trail. The trail will be on the right. This trail weaves along Sally Brook, with a sign marking it. The hike is very moderate over the soft duff of a lightly used trail. In fact the real climbing doesn't begin until 2700'. This is where the views start as well. There are a couple nice view points along the climb up, but the summit is the kicker. The top has a very nice open cliff to take in the surrounding views of the area. The best views are back toward Elk Lake and the Pinnacle Ridge. Boreas Mountain and the Hoffman Mountain range can also be seen quite clearly across the valley.

Approx. distance from Elk Lake parking: 2.5 miles
Approx. time: 3.5 to 4 hours RT

Dix Range from Sunrise Mountain

View of Elk Lake from Sunrise Mountain

#78
Stewart Mountain
Elevation 3602'
Map #26

I can't say enough about Stewart Mountain, how about I start with it has great views along the climb and along the summit ridge. Then I'll end it with a whimper. I really got beat up on this one-poked in the eye three times by dead branches, and about a 10' fall onto my back from a cliffs whose dead tree broke on me as I was pulling myself up on it. Yes all this and I wasn't even on the summit yet. But I'm sure you'll have much better luck than I did-I pray you do.

*Via Copperas Pond Trail
*Trail/Bushwhack
*Blue Route

The Copperas Pond Trail is located just east of Wilmington Notch on Rte 86. The trail starts on a hill with a steady climb of 300' in the first 0.25 miles before leveling off to the intersection with Winch Pond on the left. You will want to follow the left trail for 0.2 miles to another intersection-this is a cut off trail back to Copperas Pond. Again go left toward Winch Pond. After about 0.15 miles hiking there is an old trail that enters on the right. This trail leads back behind the ponds and comes out near Monument Falls along Rte 86. This intersection is the one you want to be at, or there about. This old trail is rarely used if at all and is beginning to get grown up; a careful eye may be needed to spot it.

Now it's time to leave the trail, split the intersection and head SE over the outlet of Winch Pond and to the southern Marsh Pond, which is less than 0.5 miles away. There will be a short up and down as you pass between to small hills. Make your way around the south side of the pond and cross its outlet, be sure to go directly E from the pond to hit the ridge that splits two drainages. The terrain here is very flat for a short stretch but soon starts a steady climb to a small knob along the ridge. This is where the spruce starts to really appear. It's not terribly thick at this point, but it's making it self very noticeable. After a short hike along a shelf you will begin to climb again, but now through a much thicker section, with many small patches of blowdown to fight through. The summit crown is very thick and strong arming these trees is what you'll need to do. This route will bring you to the southern end of the flat ridge where the views are. The views aren't from any rocky outcrop but from a mossy rise in the ridge that is free of trees; there is room for about 4 people to stand there, but not much more. You'll be able to see Sunrise Notch, Whiteface, and Lake Placid off in the distance with Moose Mountain behind it. Continue on along the ridge for about 100 yards to the true summit.

Approx. distance from Rte 86: 2.75 miles
Approx. time: 8 to 9 hours RT

*Via the North
*Bushwhack
*Green Route

This route starts along a brook between the Whiteface Mountain Ski Center and the Wilmington Notch Campsite. Start following the brook right off for about 50' and find you way to the height of land on the left.

There is an old tote road up there that can be followed for 0.5 miles. The tote road is quite wide and can be easily followed with only a couple trees down in the way-it will end at a fork in the brook. Split this fork and continue on a moderate uphill climb through very open, witch hobble forest. This will bring you to the base of a small hill and a flat shelf. Follow the shelf around to the right of the hill and climb the very edge of the shoulder, avoiding the spruce near the top. On the other side of the shoulder you will descend slightly to the site of an old beaver pond,

Climbing Stewart Mountain above old beaver pond site

which has long dried up and now only a stream flows through it. Cross this stream and the next to reach the base of Stewart. Steer clear of the col that houses this drainage as it is riddled with blowdown and boulders-some the size of a school bus. The ground is very unstable with moss and small growth growing over the rocks and boulders from the cliffs above. Many of the rock crevices are covered by years of fallen leaves, making it one of the most inhospitable sections of bushwhacking the Lower 54, and a very unsafe hiking environment. Think of it as walking through a mine field with the constant thought of loosing a leg.

The approach you should take is the direct route to the summit. There will be a few cliffs to get around and some very steep sections near the beginning of the climb, but they will soon become part of the past as you keep climbing. Be sure to look back over your shoulder as you climb and catch the views of Whiteface as they start to appear. This route offered us with very little in the way of blowdown. The route was thick but there seemed to be a lot of narrow passage ways through the woods to get us around most of it. However, the last 0.5 miles is thick, especially approaching from the direct north along the ridge. Avoid this lower section of the ridge by skirting it to the E (left) and hit the ridge from the NE. The true summit has small views and is along a flat narrow ridge, the best views are at the S end of the ridge.

Approx. distance from Rte 86: 2.1 miles
Approx. time: 7 to 8 hours RT

#79
Jay Mountain
Elevation 3600'
Map #27

Jay Mountain is one of the best hikes around and just so happens to be on the Adirondack 100 Highest list. When combined with Saddleback for an extended outing, it just doesn't get much better. Most maps show the trail through The Glen and Merriam Swamp to Grassy Notch, but this route is now private and the trail has been moved. The trail is now closer to the Town of Jay at the junction of the Jay Mountain Road and the Luke Glen Road.

Jay Ridge

*Via the State Trail
*Trail
*Blue Route

This trail all though unmarked is very easy to follow and gets a lot of attention from hikers. The trail starts out following a property line and comes to the base of a steep section at 0.5 miles. The trail continues along and goes over a few more small hills until it reaches the ridge at about 1.5 miles. There is a 360 degree view from this part of the ridge with many more to come. The next 1.5 miles is along a ridge with many views and many small bumps. You will enter the woods and come out on an open rocky ledge, many times over the course of the next hour. The summit is at the far end of the ridge and also offers 360 degree views; a rather large cairn marks the summit.

Approx. distance from road: 3 miles
Approx. time: 5 to 5.5 hours RT

*Via Saddleback Mountain
*Bushwhack
*Green Route

This is a short section of very open woods that I use when bagging both Saddleback and Jay Mountains in the same trip. I highly recommend this loop with Saddleback (see the section on Saddleback in this guide (page 176) to get details on the remaining section of the loop).

From the summit of Saddleback, descend to the N along the base of a cliff and a steep section this will quickly get you down off the mountain and on an easier terrain. You will find yourself in a very green mossy hike through very open forest. You will cross a small stream or two and go over a couple small bumps. At 0.75 miles from Saddleback you will be on one of the small bumps, and you can clearly see a bare spot on the side of Jay. This is the top of a short sandy-covered slide. Take a bearing to this spot and you'll have amazing views as well as being just below the summit of Jay. The remaining short ascent to the summit of

Jay is a combination of slab hiking and bouldering. It's that much fun. Then summits views are nice, but only half as much as the remaining section of the ridge.

Approx. distance from Saddleback: 1.3 miles
Approx time: 1 to 2 hours, one way

Jay Mountain in winter

#80
Pitchoff Mountain
Elevation 3600'
Map #28

Pitchoff Mountain can be approached on two sides via a state trail. You can reach the summit from either side, but I recommend a through hike. During the summer you can see as many as 75 cars parked near the two trailheads near Cascade Lakes. Granted a lot of these cars are from people climbing Cascade and Porter, but I would put money on the fact that only about 10% of them are doing Pitchoff. You also may notice people walking along the lakes with backpacks on; these hikers are doing the loop with only one car, walking back to the start. This adds about 2.5 miles to the trip.

*Via the South Ridge
*Trail
*Blue Route
This trail starts adjacent to the Cascade/Porter Trail; you will need to share parking. The trail quickly brings you to the top of a ridge above the lake and Rte 73. There will be a few small side trails along the ridge that will take you to some really nice lookouts. You will then drop into a small saddle at about 0.9 miles. The trail now gets steeper as it climbs the side of Pitchoff. You will notice a narrow section of loose sand and rock; this is the sight of a small rock slide. Below you will see the truck size boulder that caused the damage. The trail continues a steep ascent over eroded conditions, loose rock, and exposed roots. At 1.5 miles there is an intersection on the right that leads 0.1 miles to a large open summit and the Balanced Rocks; also referred to as the "Lemon Squeezer". Look under the Balanced Rocks for a narrow dike in the summit floor. Lower yourself down into this spot and follow it left to its end. There is a small boulder partially blocking the way, a little

maneuvering will get you over it. At the end is a huge surprise. You will be under a rock canopy on the side of the mountain. Sounds pretty cool, doesn't it? Once you're done be sure to return to the main trail and the intersection and hang a right to continue on to the summit of Pitchoff. The trail from here starts out very moderate then encounters a few steeper sections, again over eroded surfaces. The summit is wooded offering no real views. Disappointed? Well, the best views are along the other section of the ridge, which makes the loop option the most popular.

Distance from the road: 2 miles
Approx. time: 3 to 4 hours RT

*Via the North Ridge
*Trail
*Green Route

This trail begins N of the Cascade Lakes, with parking on the right. The parking area has room for a half dozen cars. Parking along the roadside is not recommended; first come first serve. You will start off on an easy grade as you cross the brook a couple times, and then the climbing begins. The terrain isn't overwhelming at first but soon becomes quite steep as you pass by a rocky bump to your right. The trail now is steep as it approaches the ridge and the first bump, at around 1.3 miles. You'll enjoy amazing views from this spot. You will continue along the ridge and go over 3 more prominent bumps; one at 1.9 miles, another at 2.3 miles and the last at 2.7 miles. Each of these summits has stellar view. You will come to the wooded summit of Pitchoff Mountain at 2.9 miles.

Distance from the road: 2.9 miles
Approx. time: 4 to 4.5 hours RT
Distance of loop, end to end: 4.9 miles
Approx. time: 5 to 5.5 hours

Along Pitchoff Ridge

#81
Saddleback Mountain
Elevation 3600'
Map #27

This is a gem of a peak, one that I have climbed many times and see myself climbing it many more. If you combine this hike with Jay Mountain, you'll have an amazing day that will be very rewarding with its open views and rocky outcrops.

*Via Bald and Slip Mountain
*Bushwhack/Trail
*Black Route

This hike was designed to extend a day trip into the Jay Range with 3 close friends. The plan was to snag Jay Mountain along the ridge after an assault on Saddleback. Jay never happened because of deteriorating weather. However, an amazing route to Saddleback was discovered.

We stashed a car early that morning near the end of the trail for Jay Mountain, in hopes of reaching it in one piece later that day. This route should be used as a two car loop because going back to your car would be a very long return hike.

Our hike started from the end of the Seventy Road located outside the Village of Lewis. The Seventy road is dirt and very narrow, but in good shape. You can reach the parking area with a car just drive carefully. The parking area is big enough for 4-5 cars, but the chance of another car being there is rare.

From the car, the hike started out as a bushwhack, no trails to warm up on with this one. We crossed the road and stepped into an open forest

176

of hardwoods. The terrain has a slight pitch up to a shoulder of a small hill, before we descended slightly to cross a branch of Hale Brook in just about 0.1 miles from the car. Soon after, Seventy Mountain came into clear view to our right. Be sure not to mistake this for Bald Mountain. Seventy is a nice mountain with nice views, but a little out of the way for this trip. The hike opened up even more as we crossed a small marshy area along a flatter stretch of woods, but the ease of low land hiking quickly came to an end as we closed in on the slopes of Bald Mountain. Bald soon started to show its features at just over 0.5 miles; with large steep slopes of moss covered rock slabs, tall ledges and a field of stinging nettles. We ended up having to negotiate one ledge with a risky climb up a natural staircase with the support of a well-anchored spruce. That's where the views began. We had amazing views back down on Hathaway Swamp and the mountain range around Fay and Little Fay Mountains. We pushed on to the summit over rock slab and scree for another couple hundred vertical feet before finally standing atop Bald Mountain at 0.65 miles. The views from the rocky summit are 360 degrees, but we had to take in different points on the ridge to get them.

The ridge up Slip was in excellent view, we could see the open woods we needed to navigate, and we were getting pretty excited about it. Bluff and Little Bluff were off to the N with their tall cliffs looming on the valley below.

From the summit of Bald we made a descent route off the N side, jumping off short ledges, switch backing others and quickly we were in the col with Slip. Tall ledges in both directions guard the col on Slip. We decided to go left in hopes of running into a chance to get through them. We found a small dike, narrowed by tall ledges on both sides and almost blocked at the top by stacked rock slabs. We did manage to top out on the cliffs by shimming our way up on the right; the first person up helped the rest of us get our footing with a strong hand. This route was a little risky; if you do decide to tackle the dike, please use extreme caution. Other ways around the ledges can be found to the right, choosing that might be advisable.

177

Slip Mountain from Bald Mountain

We were now hiking through open woods along a steep and narrow ridge. We hugged the southern edge of the ridge in hopes to grab as many views as we could, and in hopes to find more slab rock to hike on. There wasn't much for slab rock, but the views were never ending. At times we had to retreat to thicker woods only to emerge to a small lookout with a different view from the last. Our last view came at around 1.3 miles; on the last bump of the ridge just before a descent into a shallow col. The woods opened up again for the climb to the summit, only to close in for the last 100 feet. We had reached the summit at 1.75 miles from the car, having only suffered minor scarring, a field of stinging nettles, and a hornet's nest.

Saddleback Mountain

The summit offers a wide variety of views. We wandered to the SE and found grassy ledges with amazing views to the S with hawks soaring above us. But the summit boasts the most. Open rock top and amazing views toward Saddleback and Jay. We scoped out our route to Saddleback over a snack of dark chocolate and dried fruit; deciding on a descent SW to a brook that feeds the valley below. This would mean a steep descent and more of a climb than trying to navigate the ridge. We saw the ridge as being littered with bumps, and through past experiences we find that the bumps often offer the hassle of thicker woods, so avoiding them sounded like the best plan.

Our jumping off point was simple, once we figured out how to get down the cliffs we were on. We soon found ourselves in decent woods descending somewhat steeply. Once off the initial summit the woods opened up like a park. Grassy underfoot, large hardwoods, and open forest; we were in heaven. It was pretty much like this all the way to the col and the main part of the brook that leads up the flanks of Saddleback. At just under 2 miles we hit the very top of the brook; dried up from all the warm weather we had been having. The water soon appeared however, gladly accepted.

We were now approaching the col at around 2.25 miles where we were please to find a rather large two-tiered beaver pond, with old growth hardwoods standing throughout. This was truly an amazing site. We now needed to start our ascent of Saddleback as we could see and feel the weather moving in.

We followed the brook for quite some time, keeping it to our right, we rarely had to stray, and conditions were great. We only had to cross the brook when it started to meander away from where we wanted to go. That was only once and we never saw the brook again. The woods on the other side were just as pleasant as before.

Small valleys with ferns, short ledges, open hardwoods, and clear evergreen forests. The terrain then started to get steep as we approached the ridge N of the actual summit by about 0.25 miles. My

179

advice to you is trying to hit the summit as direct as possible. We found the ridge to be thick and scratchy, with the tendency to be down right miserable.

We soon found ourselves on the summit marked with a small five rock cairn. No views really to be had, except a small glance of Jay Ridge. The best views are from the lower saddle, a quick hike away; if you're interested.

From here we had the dilemma; continue over to Jay or descend off Saddleback to the road to the S. The weather was now moving in rather quickly, getting cold with a slight drizzle in the air. We decided to bail out and head for the road. When you are here you will hopefully have your day planned out a little better than us, and the decision won't be quite as hard to make. It's a nice descent to Frenyea Mountain to the S or a nice hike along the ridge to Jay. The choice is yours, and both routes are described in this guide.

Approx. Distance from Seventy Road: 3.5 miles
Approx. Time 4 to 5 hours, one way

*Via the Jay Mountain Road and Frenyea Mountain
*Bushwhack
*Red Route

This was the route we used for our first and second ascent of Saddleback. Being the easiest and most popular route, we decided it would be a good choice, turns out it is. We started this bushwhack from the height of land on the Jay Mountain Road (was named Glen Road). But the trick was getting to that spot. The road was as rough as I had ever seen. Wash boarding, pot holes, loose rocks and emerging boulders; cars with low clearance may have some trouble.

There is a small pull off at this height of land enough for about 4 cars. We parked in this usually empty parking lot. Directly across the road a small herd path can be seen, we followed this until it disappeared; which was rather quickly. The woods are very open, with practically no issues. We soon found ourselves on the steep slopes of Frenyea Mountain. In spots we needed to pull ourselves up using a well placed tree, the traction was quite unstable making the going near the top very slow. As we approached the top we found ourselves getting into thicker growth. Nettles, past their stinging phase, and old growth berry bushes, covered a few sections. Other sections were dotted with downed trees, and thicker evergreens. At around 0.35 miles from the parking lot we stood on the wooded summit of Frenyea. Not much for views, but Saddleback can be seen to the N. Actually avoiding the exact summit may be something you would want to do-the blowdown seems to be getting worse up there.

We descended slightly into the col with Saddleback before starting a steady climb up the ridge. The going is a little thick with witch hobble, and tall grass. It was very hard to see where we were stepping, and with every step we had thoughts of disturbing a hornet's nest. Never did happen, but the fear was always there. We did however find ourselves falling a few times and tripping over hidden branches. It's pretty slow going. Along the mostly open ridge there are a few flat areas that gave us relief from the bushes. Then at around 0.8 miles we started to enjoy some really nice views as rocky sections started to appear. We did have to return to the berry bushes, and witch hobble for shorter sections, but as we crested a small knoll at around 0.85 miles the terrain was much more open. Short bushes to walk through, small rocky ledges, and all sizes of rock outcropping made for an excellent hike from this point to the lower saddle. The top of the lower summit is amazing, views in many different directions; breathtaking. We had views of Slip in the NE to Lake Champlain and Vermont in the E.

The actual summit is just one bump away, and 0.1 miles. After a small descent into the saddle and a short climb through thick spruce, we were standing next to a small rock cairn on the true summit.

Approx. distance from Jay Mountain Road: 1.3 miles
Approx. time: 5 to 6 hours RT

*Via Jay Mountain
*Bushwhack
*Green Route

To get remaining route descriptions for the loop with Jay Mountain,
please see the Jay Mountain section of this guide (page 170).

Open woods between Slip Mountain and Saddleback Mountain

Sunny on lower saddle of Saddleback Mountain

#82
Pillsbury Mountain
Elevation 3597'
Map #9

Pillsbury Mountain is a nice day hike for all family members, with the reward of great views from a fire tower on this wooded summit. The porch of the closed observer's cabin next to the tower provides a nice place for a lunch or snack.

*Via the State trail from the East
*Trail
*Black Route

Follow Rte 30 out of Indian Lake and look for a dirt road just before Mason Lake, about 4 miles from the bridge over Lewey Lake. This road is called the Perkins Clearing Road. Follow it for just over 3 miles to Perkins Clearing. At the intersection take a right and this will lead you to Sled Harbor and another intersection. At this point low clearance vehicles may need to park here, and walk the remaining 1.2 miles to the trail. The trail will be located on the left, after a walk or drive over a frequently rough and ragged dirt road, which is can be tormented with wash outs and big rocks. The trail immediately drops at 0.1 miles to a crossing over the Miami River. The trail from here starts to climb and goes from steep to moderate and back again for the next mile before leveling off to a mild climb to the ridge. After this moderate section it is a relatively flat hike to the summit, at 1.6 miles. There are some views from ground level, but the best ones are found from the closed tower.

Distance from trailhead: 1.6 miles
Approx. time: 3 to 4 hours RT

184

Pillsbury Mountain fire tower

#83
Slide Mountain
Elevation 3584'
Map #29

Slide Mountain is the shortest of the Sentinel Range peaks, and possibly the easiest to summit. Either approach described below is fine, or a combination of the two would make for an amazing loop if you spot a car.

*Via South Notch
*Trail/Bushwhack
*Green Route

This abandoned DEC trail is now becoming more overgrown, but with the help of some occasional flagging, the way is apparent. To find the trail drive the River Road outside of Lake Placid for about 2 miles until you pass the Mountain Lake Academy. The trail starts just past the school on the right.

The old trail follows a brook on the right and an old dirt road for a short distance. The road will fork after a short distance; keep right and follow the brook. The trail is overgrown in spots and wet in others but very gentle. After 1.4 miles you will come to a spot in which you will need to cross the brook and head W toward the South Notch. The brook crossing in wet weather can be tricky, but in most cases it's no trouble at all. Once across the brook you will find that the trail is much less obvious-look for flagging. From here to the swampy area that lies below the notch, the flagging is pretty easy to follow through the mostly open hardwood forest. As you approach the swampy area, pass it to the left. There used to be a shelter in this area but it has been long removed, it can still be seen on some maps. The climb to the notch isn't real steep, and the woods are still generally open. Some restricted views can be had through the trees atop the notch.

From South Notch take a bearing directly N to the ridge of Slide. This section to the ridge is very steep and contains cliffs that will need to be navigated. There are many small shoots to follow that will weave you in an out of traffic, so to speak. All in all the terrain isn't overly thick. Along the way be sure to look back over your shoulder at the nice views opening up behind you. The view from just S of Slide's summit is my favorite. The summit itself offers nothing much for views; keep that in mind as you're climbing. Take in what views you can on the way up.

Approx. distance from the River Road: 4 miles
Approx. time: 6 to 7 hours RT

A view from Slide Mountain

The Other 54

*Via the Alstead Hill Road
*Trail/Bushwhack
*Blue Route

Start this hike from the end of the Alstead Hill Road located just outside of the Village of Keene. From the end of the road hike down the Jackrabbit Trail until you came to a bridge over a major outlet; about 0.75 miles from the parking lot. About a half mile up the brook there is a camping area and an outhouse-seemingly out of place. When we did this route we continued by keeping the brook to our left and climbed part way up the shoulder of Black Mountain. Doing this we needed to hike back down to the brook as the slopes got steeper and the woods a little thicker. We then crossed the brook and kept it to our right until we were in the col of Slide Mountain and Black Mountain.

In the col you will enjoy the open, spacious woods that this section of the Sentinel Range has to offer. From this point, leave the brook and head slightly N of W. Here the woods were very open, no joke, we could walk with our hand straight out to the sides and still avoid vegetation. The forest wood remain open the entire rest of the hike.

Just below the summit there is a small patch of blow down, but not enough to impede our travels. This actually has open up some views for us. The summit is feet beyond with no views.

Approx. distance from parking: 2.5 miles
Approx. time: 4 to 5 hours RT

188

#84
Gore Mountain
Elevation 3583'
Map #30

Gore Mountain is the home of a state run ski area, so as you can probably imagine the summit offers little for a wilderness experience. The fire tower that sits atop this busy summit is covered in radio and microwave antennas, and is blocked by a gate to keep curious hikers away. It's a far cry from when it was originally built back in 1918. This summit may be the most unattractive of "The Other 54", but at least the trail to it is very nice.

*Via the Snow Bowl
*Trail
*Red Route
The trail begins from Ski Bowl Road. You can find this road off Rte 28 in North Creek; just N of the 28/28N intersection.

From the parking area, climb up a small hill to the trail register, then continue steeply up a ski slope for 0.5 miles to another ski slope shortly after. The trail moderates at about 0.8 miles where it enters the woods. At just shy of 1.25 miles the trail will cross Roaring Brook and a dirt road. Soon after, you'll encounter a power line and again climb steeply. At the height of land on the shoulder of Burnt Ridge, you will descend into what's called Dave's Cirque. This is a very beautiful open hardwoods ravine and amphitheater, a very sweet spot for a break. The trail climbs moderately out of the ravine along side a rock wall and many rock formations before topping out on Paul's Ledge; another amazing spot along this climb. Just to the right is a lean-to; the sunset from here are amazing.

189

After the lean-to the trail will weave in and out of cross country ski trails and eventually downhill ski trails to one of the ski lodges at 3.4 miles. From here the trail follows a maintenance road that is steep at times, right to the summit tower. There are nice views from the summit, and the top of the ski trails-don't get me wrong. Unfortunately the sight of all the man made structures and clearings take something away from the beauty. There are great long distance views of the High Peaks.

View From Paul's Ledge

Distance from Ski Bowl: 4.5 miles
Approx. Time: 4 to 5 hours RT

*Easter Egg Hunt
*Ski Trails

There is one other nice way to climb Gore. Wait until right after the lifts close and the ski season is over. If you start near the base lodge, you'll find the runs still covered with heavy, deep snow. The snow is perfect for bare booting on a warm, sunny day. You won't posthole either. The snow here is from snow guns, and it's dense and heavy. The normal ugliness of hiking in a ski area is gone as the access roads and trails are all covered, the corn snow is great for edging and climbing, and on a sunny day, you can hike in shorts and a t-shirt on snow due to the sun and heat reflectivity. Some friends of mine enjoy hiking ski trails for this reason, and even wager a post hike adult beverage on who locates the most lost change during the hike. Since the route climbs under the ski lifts, the slowly melting snow reveals all the coins and other items that fall out of the pockets of the skiers while riding the chairlifts. This is also a much shorter route to the top than the trail. The route lengths and times very depending on which ski trail you use. The descent should be much quicker than the climb. The slopes are steep, wet and very slippery. This makes for excellent glissading conditions.

#85
Dun Brook Mountain
Elevation 3580'
Map #31

Dun Brook Mountain is the highest point along the ridge in the Fishing Brook Range. It's surrounded by private land and leased to various sportsmen's clubs. However, here's the catch; the leased land is only access, the summit isn't leased and is still private. The summit is off limits at this time to hikers (as of spring 2007). Please respect the landowner's rules and privacy, contact them before entering their property. Even though the summit is off limits I will give route descriptions on what I know. Some day the summit may have fewer limitations. We were granted permission well before the summit was considered off limits.

*Via Unnamed Peak (Fishing Brook Range) #91
*Bushwhack
*Green Route
For a description of this route please see the chapter on Unnamed Peak (Fishing Brook Range) in this guide (page 216).

*Via the Salmon Pond Club Road
*Trail/Bushwhack
*Blue Route
This approach is found off Rte. 28N/30 just north of the trailhead for Blue Mountain. The road is gated and posted, so you'll either need to be a member, guest, or be granted permission to continue. The membership is the way to go, hence saving you a 4.5 mile walk along a road. After Salmon Pond the road will enter a col with Tirrell and Tongue

Mountains before coming to a fork with a road to Wolf Pond. This is the starting point of the bushwhack.

Seeing as how we had a membership to the fish and game club; we had the privilege of driving to the intersection N of Salmon Pond. Once here, we got our act together and began our hike up the right fork toward Wolf Pond. This road ends at a gate a few hundred feet from the intersection, but that was as far as we needed to go. The end of the road was at a small clearing, making for a better place to park.

On the left of the clearing is an old woods road about the width of a small car. We used this as an approach to the ridge of Dun Brook Mountain. Following the road we encountered a few obstacles; mud, water, a few downed trees, but mostly tall ferns and grass. Along the way we found that the road may be going to far N, so we left it only to find ourselves back on it in about 100'.

The road does fork in a few spots but most of these are just detours around wet areas. Whenever we encountered a fork we went right keeping the ridge directly above us. This road became hard to follow in a few spots but we focused on the surroundings and easily kept the road under us. We noticed that the woods road stayed right below the W ridge the entire way, keeping us at a very moderate pace. Near the end of our easy hike along the road it got very narrow with bigger trees growing, but eventually turns into a path, possibly made by game.

From here we were 0.3 miles from the summit and below a very steep slope. We decided to approach the steep slope and go to the ridge; this was a little too early. I would recommend that anyone climbing this peak from the direction continue below the ridge for another 0.2 miles or so, the woods seemed to be more open further to the E.

After a very steep climb through open woods to the ridge we found ourselves in a continuously thicker forest. The ridge wasn't anything terrible but much closer quarters and many more downed trees than we had seen up to this point. The worst section we found was 0.2 miles from the summit, with very thick pines growing through downed trees.

This lasted for a while before we emerged out into a semi-open black spruce forest. The summit is fully wooded but open enough to be able to relax and eat a snack. We looked around the summit for a view; we did find a couple small ones. Looking N/NE we could see the Santanoni Range as well as the Seward Range. Further off were the MacIntyre's and Marcy.

Approx. distance from the fork in the road: 1.5 miles
Approx. time from fork in the road: 3 to 3.5 hours RT

A small road block in route to Dun Brook Mountain

#86
Noonmark Mountain
Elevation 3556'
Map #32

Noonmark Mountainhas three routes to the summit, two of which are trails and one a short bushwhack. The two trails are well traveled and the bushwhack is becoming more and more popular with signs of a herd path appearing. No matter what hike you choose, or a combination of the two, you are pretty much guaranteed a nice walk in the park, unless Mother Nature has something to say about it.

*Via the Stimson Trail
*Trail
*Blue Route

This route starts from the Ausable Club Road in St. Huberts and starts along an easement of private roads, so hikers should respect the privacy of the club. Start your hike along the private roads to a DEC sign marking the start of the foot trail. There are a number of other private roads that come in on the route, be sure to avoid these and stay on the marked route. The footpath starts at around 0.25 miles. The trail is a moderate climb to an intersection at 0.6 miles. Straight is the Dix Trail and another approach to Round Mountain. The right fork is the Stimson Trail to Noonmark.

The trail now climbs, at times very steeply, to open ledges before easing up along the ridge. After another 0.5 miles the trail begins to get steep again while going in and out of view points, and finally reaching the summit rocks. The trail then skirts the steep rocks and descends a little before finally the last steep pitch is reached just before the summit. The summit has amazing views, with the Great Range to one side of you

The upper reaches of the Stimson Trail

and the Dix Range to the other. Back to the N you will see the slides on Giant, just calling to you, "Climb me; Climb me". Well you should, it makes for another great day outside.

Distance from parking: 2.1 miles
Time: 3.5 to 4 hours RT

*Via Round Pond
*Trail
*Green Route

This trail starts off Rte 73 and follows the trail into Dix Mountain for the first 2.3 miles. You will start out climbing along a hill side at a moderate pace before coming to a height of land and a short descent to the shores of Round Pond. The hike around the pond has a tendency to be wet and muddy at any time of year. This is due to the slopes surrounding the pond and some natural springs nearby. Once around the pond you will find yourself on a moderate but steady climb up a slope to a col at 1.5 miles or about 3100'. The trail will continue over some wet areas but on mostly flat terrain to the junction with the Dix Trail from the Ausable Club Road. Here it is only a mile to the summit of Noonmark via the Felix Alder Trail.

The climb at this point starts out moderately, but will get much steeper. At 0.5 miles, you will come to the semi-open ridge of Noonmark followed by a short steep pitch to the open summit.

Distance from Rte 73: 3.3 miles
Time: 4 to 5 hours RT

*Via shoulder along Leach Trail
*Trail/Bushwhack
*Red Route

Starting again following the Ausable Club Road, this time all the way to the guard shack. From there follow the Lake Road to the Leach Trail that will be on your left. This trail goes to Bear Den, Dial and Nippletop. Stay on this trail for 1.5 miles or about 3100' in elevation. At this point you're on the shoulder Noonmark and the top of the ridge. If you start descending steeply, you've gone too far. You will know you're there when you are standing in an open field cleared by a forest fire. The scars of the fire are still very visible. The views from here are outstanding, especially those of the Great Range and Sawteeth.

The bushwhack begins here and goes along the ridge, over a few small bumps, and through what used to be an open hardwood and spruce forest. There used to be little blowdown, but with recent storms, that is changing. It's still a great route, but you might have to pick your way around a little more than in the past. You'll reach the Western face of Noonmark. Along the last ascent to the summit, it will be a rocky scramble and the steepness depends on how direct a route you want and where you choose to go up.

Approx. distance from parking: 3.75 miles
Approx. time: 4 to 5 hours RT
Approx. distance for loop with Stimson Trail: 5.9 miles
Approx. time for loop: 4 to 5 hours

#87
Mount Adams
Elevation 3540'
Map #33

Mount Adams, a mountain I can't say enough good things about, especially the views from the summit. The fire tower is now restored and safe to climb. At one time it was on the DEC axe list, but with the help of many fire tower supporters this historic piece is getting a second life.

*Via the State Trail
*Trail
*Blue Route

The trailhead for this peak can be found near Upper Works in Tahawus, just N of the Old MacIntyre Furnace. It is also the trail into Allen Mountain and Hanging Spear Falls.

Follow this trail slightly down hill to the crossing of the Hudson River. Then hike over a suspension bridge, through an open forest of evergreen to the shore of Lake Jimmy at 0.6 miles. When crossing this lake, be sure to take your time over the floating bridge. It is not in the best of conditions and slants on one end. Shortly after you cross the lake you will climb slightly uphill to a logging road and a tattered old cabin. Follow here to the right. At the top of a small hill, there will be a cairn marking the new start of the route up Adams (on the left).

The route is well used and very gentle over a soft and in spots wet trail. It soon becomes a little steeper, with a few switchbacks and short breathers along the way. There is one section of trail that I refer to as rugged. Meaning; very wet rock slab, large rocks to work your way over or around, and very steep terrain. This spot is actually harder to come back down.

Once on the summit it will be apparent that without the tower the views would be gone. Go up the steps and one of the best views in the Adirondacks begins to unfold.

Approx. distance from Tahawus: 2 miles
Approx. time: 4 to 5 hours RT

Calamity Mountain from Mount Adams

*Via Popple Hill
*Trail/Bushwhack
*Green Route

I wouldn't even begin to recommend this route to anyone, it was a route we did back in 2001 and has scared us for life. Not really, but I do remember a lot of swearing and talking to ourselves. We started from the same point as the above route and followed it past the point in which the trail for Adams branches off. We continued along the gravel road for another 0.5 miles to another old logging road, this one overgrown. We followed this old logging road through 6' tall blackberry bushes to another that came in on the right. This one was wet in spots and just as overgrown as the other, but this one led us to the base of Popple Hill.

The woods started out very open on the slopes of Popple Hill but we found ourselves too far to the S of the true summit along the ridge. We started to see a lot of blowdown along this ridge, and the ridge to the E of us was totally demolished. We had no choice but to drop below the ridge and skirt the blowdown. We dropped to the E side, but only slightly, just enough to avoid it and not find ourselves in another batch in the col. This worked great until we were forced back up to the ridge and on a small bump below the true summit.

From here we couldn't believe what we saw, and to this day it is the worst blowdown patch we have ever encountered. Our choices were to abort Popple Hill and Adams, or dive right in. We dove in. It took us over an hour to go the next 0.2 miles to the summit of Popple Hill. There were trees piled on trees that were on yet another layer of trees that had three others below it. At times we were walking along downed trees that were 10' in the air. We both fell off a tree or two landing on our back. To make things worse was the second growth trees. They were growing among the downed trees and very close together at that. Once through the blowdown field and just below the wooded summit of Popple, we wondered what the S face of Adams was going to be like. It was a walk in the park compared to what we just went through.

201

From the summit of Popple Hill we descended slightly to the ridge, which was relatively flat for a distance, and than climbed steadily through an evergreen forest, covered in very soft duff. There were age old trees lying covered and half decomposed from a thick layer of moss. This side of Adams is practically untouched, we felt almost guilty treading here; so remote, so old, so fragile. There were small sections of old blowdown but we easily skirted most of those. The woods weren't too thick and scratchy, but I do seem to remember a few deep cuts on my legs, maybe from stepping over a dead tree. We picked up the trail just feet from the tower. Needless to say we followed the trail back out to the car.

Approx. distance from Tahawus: 3 miles
Approx. time: 5 to 6 hours, one way
Approx. distance for loop: 5 miles
Approx. time for loop: 7 to 8 hours

The devastation on Popple Hill

#88
Fishing Brook Mountain
Elevation 3540'
Map #34

This is the mountain that is furthest N on the Fishing Brook Ridge, and is also surrounded by private land. The Salmon Pond Club is to the S, and the Minerva Fish and Game Club is to the N. Please respect the landowners by joining the club, going in as a guest, or obtaining permission before trampling the woods on their property.

*Via Unnamed Peak (Fishing Brook Range) #91
*Bushwhack
*Red Route

The distance between Fishing Brook Mountain and Fishing Brook peak is just less than 2 miles with numerous small bumps along the way. The tricky part is avoiding the thick spots. This will require you at times to drop off to the E side of the ridge but not as far as to get on the steep side hill. Go off just enough to avoid the thicker spruce. The spruce thickets are sporadic, and there are more open sections than not. At 0.1, 0.4, 0.8, and 1 mile, you'll hit small bumps before the final descent to the col with Fishing Brook Mountain. You will end up loosing roughly 375' in elevation, and then gain 450' on the climb back up to the summit. There are a few cliffs on this side of Fishing Brook Mountain that you will need to avoid. The summit views are lacking, but the steep slopes again open up some views back to the S.

Approx. distance from #91: 1.8 miles
Approx. time: 1.5 to 2 hours, one way

*Via the Minerva Club Road
*Trail/Bushwhack
*Black Route

The start of this trail follows a restricted road maintained by the Minerva Fish and Game Club. You'll need to become a member, or get permission for access. The restricted road is at the W end of the parking area between Long Lake and Newcomb, off Rte 28N.

We had gone in looking to obtain membership information by running into a member of the club and at the same time ask permission to climb. We managed to do both. About 0.5 miles in, we ran into a gentleman clearing the road and struck up a conversation. We asked him about becoming a member, how much it costs, who we need to contact, etc. He was very helpful and gave us all the information we needed. When we told him of our hiking interest, our new friend broke out a map of the property and said "sure, you can be my quests". I won't mention his name for obvious reasons, but we couldn't have run into a nicer man.

From here this road continues to a split, we went right and then shortly a left to an old, fairly large building. In the clearing there is an old woods road on the left, we followed this to another large clearing. In this clearing we ate a few raspberries and chose to take the woods road straight ahead, it got us where we were going but our route down was much better. The descent route returned us to a woods road to the back left of the clearing. It's hard to see as the tree branches cover its appearance. Preferring this route, I will present it here as an ascent route.

Follow the above mentioned road at the left of the clearing. Any time you come to an intersection, always stay on the main road, which is pretty obvious. Follow this road to what looks like its end, or at least, to the height of land. From here start a bushwhack up the shoulder of the peak. You're less than a mile from the summit at this point. The woods from here are open hardwoods with a mixture of witch hobble and ferns. The only tight spots were near the summit crown which is circled by a small cliff that can easily be climbed in a couple spots or skirted. The summit was wooded making it difficult to find the true summit. I know we were on it, because we circled the entire top and stepped on every small rise there, and confirmed it with the GPS. The GPS kept leading us back to this spot. The summit has hardly any sign of man's presence, just one small stomped area and footpath.

Our route up was a maze of woods roads, and few thicker spots along the way. Follow our route down as explained above as an ascent route and you will have a nice easy trip; almost guaranteed. We were on top at 11am. With an 8:15am start, we spoke with the member for at least 15 minutes and we were back to the car at 2pm. This included almost forty five minutes on the summit.

From the looks of the ridge near the top, completing all three Fishing Brook Range peaks in a day would be a battle. I feel it's a much better idea to do this one separately from the N and the other two from the S. It's not that it can't be done, because it has, as you can see from my route descriptions in this book.

For more information on this mountain range see the chapters on Dun Brook Mountain (page 192) and Unnamed Fishing Brook Peak (page 216) in this guide.

Approx. distance from Rte 28N: 4 miles
Approx. time: 6 to 7 hours RT

A view through the trees in the Fishing Brook Range

#89
Little Santanoni Mountain
Elevation 3500'
Map #35

This could either be a long hike or a really long trip, your choice. For example; you could walk the entire trip and total up around a 20 mile day. Or you can mountain bike on the portion of the road that leads to the Great Camp Santanoni. Or, get a carriage ride in to just S of Moose Pond; an interesting alternative. I'll provide a brief description of the entire route, so you can have a clear picture of the entire thing, whichever option you choose. Just think of it this way. Little Santanoni is the Allen Mountain of "The Other 54".

*Via the SW Ridge
*Trail/Bushwhack
*Red Route

The Santanoni Preserve is located within the Town of Newcomb and the parking is found just down a short dirt road W of Lake Harris. Park near the gatehouse and start your trip along the dirt road toward Newcomb Lake.

On this day we took advantage of a carriage ride into the Moose Pond area, we started at 7am in a light rain and me with no jacket. The ride was pleasant with no surprises from the horses, if you know what I mean. At 1 mile, we passed the old buildings of the farm and the ruins of the dairy barn that burned a few years back. Shortly after that was the now overgrown field that was once the orchard. The remaining road is mostly uphill to the intersection at 2.3 miles. At the intersection we continued our ride along a much narrower road for another 2.5 miles to a turn around spot. The worst part of this section is: it's mostly downhill, meaning we need to climb this on the way out. Why? Our carriage was unavailable for the return trip.

From here it was time to tie up our hiking boots and press on. We were soon in an open area with marsh to our left. The horse trail now went up hill for the most part with a couple smaller downhill treks. Once at the intersection with Moose Pond, we took the trail to the right around the pond. After about 0.6 miles from the intersection there is a bridge over a marshy outlet. It's a very pretty spot. The remaining trek to Ermine Brook was very easy, as was the crossing.

We started our bushwhack about 100 feet past the brook and well before the next brook crossing shown on the map. The thing is that the woods were amazingly open, so we dove in and started our climb.

Immediately we started to climb pretty steep, then it moderates to a steady climb through open hardwoods. After about 0.5 miles we came to a small shelf that had a really old overgrown road through it. This showed us how nicely nature can overcome a wound and heal itself.

From here we were now only a mile from the summit, but totally soaked from the wet trees and constant drizzle. We stood just below a small bump along the ridge, we ended up skirting the actual summit to avoid any possible thick sections, it worked out rather well there were no thick sections. Our plan was to follow the ridge all the way to the summit, so we did. The going was ever more open than lower on the mountain. There are large sections of tall ferns that seemed to weave in and out from the open forest, which was what we had to deal with; a very pleasant walk in the park if I do say so myself. We encountered thicker woods starting at around 3100', as well as heavier rain. The ridge up is straightforward though, we had little difficulty finding the true summit. A map and compass was always an option, but a paper map in a steady rain would soon become a mess.

Less than two hours from the trail we stood on the summit, as a group of 7; six with two legs and one with four. Standing on top eating a quick snack, still in a steady rain we had an almost terrifying thought. We were 9 miles from the car, a longer distance than if we were standing atop

Moose Marsh

Allen Mountain. Also, how long would it rain and could we possibly get any wetter than we were already? Well that would be soon answered. It rained for 80% of the trip out, and the crossing of Ermine Brook was now a river. Since all of us being totally soaked already we opted to walk right through it. So, that was our trip; what's your going to sound like?

Approx. distance from Preserve parking: 9 miles
Approx. time: 12 to 13 hours RT
Approx. distance from end of carriage ride: 4.25 miles
Approx. time: 6 to 7 hours RT

#90
Blue Ridge (Blue Mtn.)
Elevation 3497'
Map #36

You can climb this mountain without hitting private land. You can either from the N via the Wilson Pond Trail, or from the E via the Northville/Placid Trail. However the shortest route is via a restricted path into Dishrag Pond to the S. It's over privately owned lands and permission must be obtained before using the trail. This peak can be combined with another Blue Ridge on the list (#99). See the chapter on Blue Ridge #99 for route description of the entire ridge (page 239).

*Via Dishrag Pond Trail
*Trail/Bushwhack
*Red Route
The trail starts on the N side of Brown's Brook off the Cedar River Road in Indian Lake. You will soon leave the shore of Brown's Brook for higher ground, and then just as quickly, it begins to return to the brook. After 1.1 miles the brook splits and the trail goes right in between the two. Continue to follow the trail until it again reaches the S banks of Brown's Brook. Cross here and start a pretty straightforward bushwhack to the summit.

The banks start out very steep and pretty much remain so until the last 50 feet before the summit. There are some cliffs to avoid along this entire side of the mountain, but easily manageable. You will climb 1100' in under a mile. The summit crown is somewhat thick with small patches of blowdown. The summit views are a little lacking but the entire ridge does offer a few off both sides.

Approx. distance from Cedar River Road: 2.5 miles
Approx. time: 4.5 to 5 hours RT

*Via Wilson Pond Trail
*Trail/Bushwhack
*Black Route

The trail starts about 3 miles W of Blue Mountain Lake off Rte 28. We started out with a small climb along a very nice trail before flattening out and coming to Grassy Pond at 0.5 miles. Soon after leaving the shores of Grassy Pond we started an early assault on our days elevation gain. Along this trail we crossed over marshy areas, climbed along small ridges and skirted small bumps. Each section seems to change in atmosphere as it meanders closer to Wilson Pond. We ended up going

Fernwhacking on Blue Ridge #90

Wilson Pond

all the way into Wilson Pond to check it out, what a wonderful little spot to sit and relax. It even afforded us a small glimpse of the mountain ahead.

From the pond we retraced our steps to an outlet, which was about 0.2 miles back down the trail. This is where we left the trail and started our bushwhack. We took a bearing on the GPS of almost dead S so we could hit the small bump that lays SW of Wilson Pond. The woods were very open, in fact just a couple hundred feet off the trail we came upon a small herd path that led us around the small cliffs we encountered on this side. The top of this little bump is just under 0.25 miles from the trail. It is open hardwoods layered with a field of ferns and tall grass, very pretty.

From here we could see the ridge, so we took another bearing straight at it and began a fairly sizeable descent. The descent proved to be a little challenging with the trees getting a little close in spots, proving once again that marshy, wet areas have thicker bands of trees. After a small flat section, we were again in open hardwoods. The climb was moderate for a great distance but we knew we had a steeper section coming up, at around 2830'. We must have hit this section just right because we had no resistance from the trees at all, and even the steep section was short and sweet.

This bump along the ridge again is open but on the descent down to the next col we were not so fortunate. This was the thickest part of the day, the evergreens are entangled and we had to push our way through. Fortunately this doesn't last long, and it peters out. In fact it was only about 50'-100' of this stuff, and we were in a col that was covered in a mossy rug, very pleasing to the eye. There's about a 25' drop in elevation into this col, which we quickly regained on the other side. Once we climbed out of the col we discovered to our pleasure, that it was flat and very open in yet another grove of hardwoods. This flat section was a real treat, and a great way to make up some lost time, since the 90+ degree heat was slowing us down.

The next section we had mapped out was to deliver us to another very small rise on the ridge; a perfect place to take a breather before a steep climb to the summit ridge. This section was a piece of cake with moderate terrain, open woods, a slight breeze in the air, and soft footing. Who could ask for more?

We were now at the base of the steep section with a small rocky, mossy, incline that has a well used game path up the right of it. This got us to the top of the steep band and to a pretty decent view back to the N. The woods here started to change; they went from hardwoods to scratchy pine, back to hardwoods all the way to the summit ridge. Once on the flat of the ridge we could see that going for the NW lower bump could be a hassle, as the woods looked thick and full of blowdown. We weren't 100% sure of this, but we didn't want to see first hand either.

As a group we decided to stay below the ridge where the woods were open and head straight for the summit. This route took us through a very open old pine forest. While the summit was lacking in views, there are some through the trees. The top is also covered in blowdown, with only a small stomped out section on the exact summit. So, in that we descended via our route up and celebrated a great hike with a cold brew back at the parking area.

Approx. distance from Rte 28: 5 miles
Approx. time: 7 to 8 hours RT

#91
Unnamed Peak (Fishing Brook Range)
Elevation 3480'
Map #31

This is the middle or connector peak to the threesome in the Fishing Brook Range. It lays N of Dun Brook Mountain and S of Fishing Brook Mountain. There are many small bumps along the ridge but the true summit lies right in the middle. This mountain is on private land, as are the two surrounding it. Please obtain permission to hike there.

*Via Fishing Brook Mountain
*Bushwhack
*Red Route
See the chapter on Fishing Brook Mountain in this guide (page 203).

*Via Dun Brook Mountain
*Bushwhack
*Green Route
The traveling is mostly open woods with the exception of the tops of the smaller bumps. When we ran into thicker woods we left the ridge to the E, but not as far as the steeper slopes. You will see, as we did, that you will end up following the E side of the ridge for most of the hike.

From the summit of Dun Brook we headed N along the ridge and descended about 300' to the col. The going was quite open for most of this section except for a patch in the col, we headed to the E to avoid as much as possible. We were now in an open black spruce forest, and then it soon started to mix with hardwoods making for a much more pleasant hike. We avoided the actual summit of the first bump along the ridge by skirting it to the E avoiding the obvious thicker woods. The next decent was quite sizable to the col with another major bump. After this was the start of the climb to the top of Fishing Brook Peak. The woods in the col we found to be very open with scattered fields of ferns and the climb just as pleasant. Don't attack this peak straight on, as it is pretty thick and looks very unforgiving. The top was an open spruce forest with an open hardwoods forest on the other side. The ridge from here was a couple ups and downs, much like the other sections along the ridge. Just remember when the going gets tough, the tough get going to the E.

The summit of this peak is much like the other summits in this range, a whole lot of nothing. A few ribbons marked this summit, so no searching around was required. Those ribbons may or may not be there for future climbers to find.

Below was our route off the mountain but I will explain it as an approach instead, for those wishing to do only this peak.

Approx. distance from Dun Brook Mountain: 1.6 miles
Approx. time: 1.5 to 2 hours, one way

*Via the beaver pond to the Southwest
*Trail/Bushwhack
*Black Route

Start this hike from the same intersection as mentioned above but go up the left fork rather than the right. This road can actually be driven with a higher clearance vehicle for a ways further. There will be a washed out culvert stopping you short of the beaver pond. At the beaver pond continue to follow the road, now very overgrown with tall grass and raspberry bushes. Along the way are very wet sections that need to be hopped and skirted as well as a few small brooks crossing, but most of the road is easily traveled. There are a few small intersections with other overgrown woods roads. Be sure to keep to the left and you will be on the route. You'll need to leave the road before its end, which is about 0.5

miles from the beaver pond.

You will now have to leave the woods road and start an easy, open bushwhack to the summit. The woods are a mix of hardwoods and witch hobble, with the witch hobble being the trying part. It always seems to trip you at the knees. The slopes are quite steep and steady with a couple of small cliffs to skirt. At around 0.25 miles from the summit, the spruce starts to reappear.

This route combined with the one above and the climb up Dun Brook, make for a great day's loop, highly recommended if you need both peaks.

Approx. distance from the intersection: 1.75 miles
Approx. time: 1.5 to 2 hours, one way
Approx. distance for loop: 4.9 miles
Approx. time for loop: 6.5 to 7 hours

#92
Puffer Mountain
Elevation 3472'
Map #37

Just S of Chimney Mountain lays the untrailed summit of Puffer Mountain. The cool water of Puffer Pond sets nestled to the N shadowed also by Bullhead Mountain. There are two approaches to the summit of Puffer, both of which are good approaches and one of which could grow up much thicker in a few years. Read below and choose your poison, or make a loop of the two. Both start and finish from the same spot; Kings Flow.

*Via the Kings Flow Trail from the West
*Trail/Bushwhack
*Green Route

Our group met early on this morning in hopes of discovering something new. Three close friends, and two dogs, soon to be friends. From the field at Kings Flow we followed the trail on the E side of Kings Flow along an old jeep/ATV trail, turned hiking trail. The going is very flat along a sometimes wet and muddy trail. At about 1 mile the trail forks with a herd path to the right. This appears to be a fisherman's path down to the water. From the intersection the trail goes uphill steadily, and then flattens out again for a short distance before coming to a major intersection to our right. The trail to the right cuts back W very sharply; in fact we didn't even see this intersection on the way in. We continued slightly down hill to the shore of Puffer Pond Brook, where we easily found a place to cross. From the stream we started our climb up the slopes of Puffer. Its gradient is quite moderate through open forest, until we came to a steep section with mossy ledges and slippery footing. In fact on one small section it was a group effort, one relying on another for a hand. Along this section there were nice views of Bullhead and Kings

219

Flow. After a steep climb of 600' in the first 0.5 miles we were on the W ridge. Up to this point we encountered very little resistance, the woods were generally open.

Along the ridge we found many small open sections of what looked to be fields of ferns. Being early spring, it was hard to tell. Ferns don't tend to thrive during Indian Lake's sub-zero winters. However, the coolest thing we saw was a couple very large sections of young growth evergreens. These may grow up to be very thick sections for future bushwhackers. Keep an eye out from here to the summit. Moose tracks and dropping were very abundant along the entire stretch; there could be a good chance of spooking one. We finally hit the summit after a couple hours of climbing. We had hopes for some kind of view, but they didn't appear. The top was fully wooded. On the bright side, it was very peaceful to have the entire summit to ourselves.

Approx. distance from Kings Flow: 2.9 miles
Approx. time: 5.5 to 6 hours RT

Along Kings Flow

*Via Puffer Pond from the North
*Trail/Bushwhack
*Blue Route

This trail also starts from Kings Flow but leaves the parking area to the W. You will quickly cross a bridge and not long after start a gradual uphill climb. At about 0.75 miles in you will come to Carroll Brook which can be tricky to cross, depending on how much mischief the beavers have been up to lately. Once across the brook you will follow its shores for 0.2 miles before you turn away and start a rather steep climb to the shoulder of Bullhead Mountain. From here you will lose 200' in elevation to the shore of Puffer Pond and its lean-to. The trail forks here; go right to the SW end of the pond.

It will be a little over 0.3 miles to the end of the pond where you will need to start to look for a crossing of the ponds outlet. From here the climb starts immediately, moderate at first, but quickly becomes quite steep and steady. The woods are quite open for the most part, but some periodic downed trees will slow the pace a little. There are numerous cliffs to battle as well. At around 2950' in elevation some small cliffs will start to appear, most of which can be easily dealt with. There will also be some quite large cliffs that need to be skirted. Nearing the top, it really gets steep and a little scratchy from the close knit trees in the area. The top is just beyond the steep slopes.

Approx. Distance from Kings Flow Parking: 3.5 miles
Approx. time: 5.5 to 6 hours RT

#93
Sawtooth #4
Elevation 3460'
Map #13

 This peak is the loneliest of the 5 Sawtooth Mountains, hence making it much easier to do it by itself. The Sawtooth Range has some of the densest forest in the NE United States, but #4 seems to be a little kinder than the others.

*Via Ward Brook Trail
*Trail/Bushwhack
*Blue Route

A couple of us started out for the Sawtooth Range in a very warm morning. In fact it would end up reaching 95 degrees that day. We followed the Blueberry Trail for about 4 miles to the Ward Brook Truck Trail. It's mellow but tends to be quite muddy in a few select areas. Please try to avoid widening the trail in these wet spots, use the rocks and logs that are laid out to cross on. At the Ward Brook Truck Trail we went left instead of the usual right toward the Seward's Trail. There is a sign that says this road leads to private property. Don't worry; you will leave the road well before the private property line. We hiked about 0.1 miles to a brook crossing and then up a small hill. On the right we saw a small clearing, which looked to be a turn around spot for a jeep or the beginning of a small road. We dove into the woods here. Just inside the woods off the road there is an unmarked trail that leads right, don't follow it, it leads away from the mountain.

The forest is quite open off the road with only minor deadfall to avoid. The first 0.5 miles are flat with the smallest upgrades, the climb starts from here on. We decided to take a bearing to a small summit S of Sawtooth #4, whose elevation is around 2500'. There were some nice views from the top of the cliffs; the Seward's look almost close enough to touch. From the top of this small knob we descended very slightly to another flat area along the ridge, where the woods were surprisingly open through a mixed forest of mostly hardwoods.

After this flat area there was another small climb to a shelf with more nice views of the Seward's. To the E we could see a small marsh so we avoided it to the W and started a much more serious climb to the summit. Fortunately the woods stayed quite open up to about 0.2 miles from the summit. This is where we encountered some extremely thick spruce. Luckily it lasted only a few hundred feet, and the woods again opened up, delivering us to a steep section below a rock ledge. We skirted our way up along the side the rock slab and perched ourselves on a gorgeous, nearly 360 degree view. The true summit was only 0.1 miles away now, and only a few feet higher. The woods weren't too dense along this summit ridge but they were nothing like the open stroll we had earlier, either. The views were quite nice, a little hazy this day, but on a clear day the other Sawtooths and the entire Seward Range can be captured.

Approx. distance from parking lot: 6 miles
Approx. time: 9 to 10 hours RT

#94
Sawtooth #5
Elevation 3460'
Map #38

Sawtooth #5 was the final summit of the Adirondack 100 Highest list for three of us on July 1ˢᵗ, 2006. It had been a long battle with, terrain, fatigue, bugs, the elements and Mother Nature but we finally finished. We kept hearing #5 is a nice peak to finish on; "it's easy" they said. Well we didn't know what to think, none of the other 4 Sawtooth Mountains have been described as "easy". Well, come to find out, it wasn't too bad. It's a short bushwhack from the Ward Brook Trail, and the woods were fairly unforgiving.

*Via the Ward Brook Truck Trail
*Trail/Bushwhack
*Red Route

With a small group of our friends joining us we again followed the well used Ward Brook Foot Trail all the way past the Blueberry Lean-to to the Ward Brook Truck Trail. This time though we continued to the right and followed it 1.75 miles to the jumping off point for Sawtooth #5. This point is roughly 0.25 miles past the twin lean-to's called Camp 4. A small sand pit marks the spot we left the trail.

The bushwhack from here started very steep over the sandy hill to a moderate climb through decently open woods. As on all other Sawtooth Peaks there is a bunch of fallen stuff to step over as we made our way to an outlet of the Sawtooth Range at 0.75 miles from the trail. We crossed this outlet at the site of an old logging bridge, now looking like downed trees over a brook. But, upon closer inspection it was obvious their purpose, with straight cuts at the edges. Once on the other side the real ascent began; we climbed roughly 700' in the next 0.3 miles.

We weaved our way through the ever growing thicker evergreens to find our "Path of the Least Resistance". We did quite well, but as usual the woods tighten up, and our pace was slowed. The woods continued to be pretty nice for over 85% of the trip; only small patches of thick bush slowed us down. On the map we noticed this peak has two very similar summits, but the one furthest away to the N will be the higher of the two.

We know found ourselves on the last 0.1 miles of the summit ridge, in open black spruce forest. We stopped, let our friends get to the top before us to take pictures, we had to get changed. Alan had the bright

View from just below summit of Sawtooth #5

idea to wear white button down shirts and ties. Well, I don't have a white shirt. Needless to say, there were two guys wearing white shirts and ties and one wearing a tie over a dirty, sweaty t-shirt. Quite the nice ending to a long adventure, I wouldn't change a thing; except maybe a view. To our disappointment there are no panoramic views but with a little looking around we were able to find some viewpoints.

I think the key to climbing this peak is to not go to far past Camp 4. We have friends who have ventured well past to try the peak and have found nothing but resistance from step one all the way to the summit. I guess that goes to show just how different it can be just a small ridge over, or even a few hundred feet.

Approx. Distance from parking lot: 7.25 miles
Approx. time: 8 to 10 hours RT

Sawtooth #5 from a marsh

<h1>#95
Wolf Pond Mountain
Elevation 3460'
Map #39</h1>

This peak has a few route options for climbing. One involves being a guest at the Elk Lake Lodge, and the other being a member of a sportsman's club. The approach my group took on this day was the one described below. We found it very pleasant and asked ourselves "why go at it any other way?" Again, the approach below is over privately leased land by a large sportsman's club. The summit is owned by Elk Lake Lodge. We obtained permission by a long-standing member to hike the road back in and bushwhack it from the S. Remember, if you aren't a member or guest, stay at the Elk Lake Lodge and climb Wolf Pond Mountain from there.

*Via Gulf Brook Road
*Road/Bushwhack
*Red Route

The Gulf Brook Road is not labeled as such on any maps, but near the gate a sign marks it as so. You can find this access off the Blue Ridge Road outside of North Hudson. There is no where to park along the Gulf Brook Road; you will need to park off the side of the Blue Ridge Road and hike up to the gate. The gate is about 200 feet off the main road and this is where your adventure begins.

The road is very well maintained and flows over rolling hills. You will pass below a rocky ridge appropriately named, Ragged Mountain. At 1.75 miles you will come to a major intersection at which point you proceed left around the S side of the mountain to the SW side for a great approach. At around 2.25 miles start looking for an old logging road off the right hand side. There is a small sand pile dumped in front of the road to stop future traffic. The road is a little obscure here, but once you're on it, it will be obvious. Follow this road to what looks to be an old clearing filled with grass and ferns. There is a small stream running through it, making this a very wet area. Continue on through this field for about 0.25 mile, the road makes a slight turn uphill. This is where we left the trail to start a bushwhack through a hardwood forest. There's not much to get in your way, only a few small sections downed trees. The last 0.1 miles to the summit was pretty thick and you'll find yourself doing the usual swimming-through-thick-spruce stoke. Luckily the trees are not tall, making for some really nice views.

The summit has very limited views; in fact there wasn't even a whole lot of room to even sit down. You might want to eat lunch below the summit in a semi-open black spruce forest, like we did.

Our descent was a little further to the E, but the woods were just as open as the climb. I would almost put money on the fact that most of the S side of this peak has nice woods at lower elevations. I emphasize "most" because in bushwhacking, 50' to one side or the other could be the difference between open and a fence of evergreens.

Approx. distance from the Blue Ridge Road: 3.5 miles
Approx. Time: 6 to 7 hours RT

View along Wolf Pond Ridge

Open woods in the valley

#96
Cellar Mountain
Elevation 3447'
Map #40

The descriptions for Cellar Mountain will be real quick, as was the hike. The round trip for us was only about a mile; thanks to a woods road and four-wheel drive. To locate the old jeep road for Cellar, drive down the Cedar River Road past Wakely Dam, it will be 3.4 miles on the right. If your vehicle has high clearance you should be ok to get a little ways up the road. We got as far as we could, about 0.5 miles, before a washout and a downed tree got in our way. But with all the crazy weather we've been having, the road may not let you get that far. The worst case scenario is; you will have to hike the extra 0.6 miles to where my route description starts. The road would be a very easy hike, as all old jeep roads are.

Usual parking along the jeep road

*Via the East Slope
*Road/Bushwhack
*Green Route

Depending on how far you get in by vehicle you may need to walk the jeep road for a little while. We did but for only about 0.1 miles. At 2800' in elevation we took our bearing toward the summit.

The woods are filled with deciduous trees on steep slopes. You'll find yourself climbing 900' in 0.3 miles. The first 0.1 miles is mellow through a forest of smaller saplings, which will get larger by the year. Then at 2950' the terrain gets very steep and a little unstable underfoot. By the time you break 3050' the slopes are relentless and some "four legged" action may be needed. Grab a tree or two to help with balance-we did. Now at 0.5 miles from the top the woods flatten out again and you can stand up straight.

Not much to see of course, but it's quiet and peaceful on the top none the less. Just through the trees you can see parts of Wakely Mountain, but not much other than that can be made out. The summits views are little better during the fall, when leaves don't obstruct the views.

Approx. distance from the Cedar River Road: 0.9 miles
Approx. time: 2 to 3 hours RT

*Via the North Ridge
*Road/Bushwhack
*Red Route

The North Ridge is excellent if you want to do a small loop. Just continue hiking the jeep road for another 0.25 miles to 2930'. This is a great jump off spot to head up the slopes to the ridge. By starting higher, the going is never to steep but it will get your heart pumping. The woods once again are very open up to just below the ridge approximately 0.2 miles from the jeep road. The woods at this point are never really thick-just a little scratchy. The black spruce forest has taken over and you are now on the ridge. There are two small bumps along this ridge between you and the summit. One is at 0.35 miles which is more of a large flat area covered with trees. The second is at 0.45 miles, this one a little more prominent than the first. This bump is actually more of a large rock covered in moss. To get to this point you will have to skirt a small patch of blowdown between bump #1 and #2. A good reason for going this way though is this patch of blowdown has made a nice view point along the ridge, and the only real chance for a photo.

From bump #2 the summit can be seen less than 0.1 miles away. From here it's really hard to tell which is higher when standing on either. Most maps show both of them on the same contour line-but it's that half a contour line that makes this summit just a bit higher.

Approx. distance from Cedar River Road: 1.4 miles
Approx. time: 3.5 to 4 hours RT
Approx. distance of loop: 2.3 miles
Approx. time of loop: 3.5 to 4 hours

#97
Blue Ridge Mountain (Schroon Lake)
Elevation 3440'
Map #41

The best way to do this peak is by combining it with Hoffman Mountain, plan a traverse through to a second car spotted either on the Hoffman Road in Schroon Lake or the Blue Ridge Road in North Hudson. It will still be a very long and grueling day, but you would have two peaks and will make a little more sense than an out and back. The only catch is the best exit or approach to Blue Ridge is through privately owned land, leased to a local hunting club. This private road can be found off the Blue Ridge Road in North Hudson, about 4.5 miles from I-87 on the left. Please get permission before you use their road as access.

Our through hike got held up during an electrical storm and a GPS failure; this pushed us off the W side of the mountain into the drainage that lead to these private roads.

*Via Hoffman Mountain
*Bushwhack
*Green Route
Please see Hoffman via Blue Ridge in the Hoffman Chapter of this guide (page 146).

*Via the North Ridge
*Road/Bushwhack
*Red Route
After our hasty exit off Blue Ridge in a summer thunderstorm we did a

little research and discovered a family member who belongs to the club and we returned as his guest. Please be sure to get permission or become a member before using this route I lay before you.

Aber Brook is the water source that the private road I mention leads to. The road will continue to follow the brook for a brief amount of time, but soon starts to veer away. The upper portion of the road is pretty open and easy to follow. A few scattered pieces of down fall to crawl under, but mostly pretty easy. Once you leave the road at roughly 1.1 miles you will be in very open woods, scattered with rocky outcrops, but climbing steadily to the ridge.

Along the ridge you will see Spruce Mountain to your left, be sure not to mistake this for a bump along the ridge. Along the ridge the woods are open, but more deadfall starts to appear, slowing the pace down a little.

Blue Ridge #97

The ridge continues on a steady climb through open to thick forest and back again. At around 1.75 miles the route gets very steep and unstable. Be very careful there are a lot of holes covered in a fine layer of moss just waiting for some unfortunate "sole" to step on.

At about 2880' the ridge comes to a small bump just below the true summit. This bump marks the start of a much harder climb. Once off the small summit you will descend to a col that's pretty open, but as soon as the climbing begins the woods start to close in. Once on the upper portion of the summit ridge there will be a few views and the summit is about 0.15 miles away through a thicker section.

From here you can see parts of Hornet Cobbles, sections of the Dix Range and West Blue Ridge, a peak very close to being in the Adirondack 100 Highest. The summit doesn't offer much for views, or a place to sit and eat. But look on the bright side, you can check out those views as you push your way back down the mountain to your car.

Approx. distance from the Blue Ridge Road: 2.75 miles
Approx. time: 7 to 8 hours RT
Approx distance for through hike with Hoffman: 9 miles
Approx time for through hike: 9 to 10 hours

#98
Morgan Mountain
Elevation 3440'
Map #42

 Morgan is possibly the easiest of the Adirondack 100 Highest with less than a 0.2 mile bushwhack that starts with an easy hike along a well used trail. There are some nice views to be had, but a little exploring may be necessary to find them.

*Via the Cooper Kill Pond Trail
*Trail/Bushwhack
*Blue route

You can find this trail in the Stephenson Range, N of Whiteface Mountain. As you drive up the Memorial Highway to Whiteface Mountain's toll booth, take a right at the fork. Left goes to the toll booth and right goes toward Franklin Falls. The trailhead for Cooper Kill Pond is about 0.25 miles past the fork.

We started our hike on the trail which initially is an old jeep/4-wheeler trail and is quite flat with very little elevation change for the first 0.5 miles. Then we started to climb moderately through the Stevenson Range while checking out the woods along the trail to see just how thick the woods are in this area. They looked pretty good, but we knew we could walk through anything for the 0.2 miles to Morgan's summit. The trail soon turns rocky and a little steeper as we approached a height of land at 1.85 miles.

Whiteface and Esther Mountains from Morgan's cliffs

Now it was time to jump in and find the top of this peak. The woods are very open so we moved quite easily through them. There was very little dead fall to step over, and very few trees to get in our way. Within 15 minutes we were on the summit. The views are only obscured ones-unless you descend slightly along the SW ridge to a very nice open ledge. We had found this ledge on a previous trip and the views of Whiteface and Esther from it are very unique.

Approx. distance from trailhead: 2.1 miles
Approx. time: 2.5 to 3 hours RT

#99
Blue Ridge (Raquette Lake)
Elevation 3436'
Map #43

The twin Blue Ridges are very inviting, especially on paper, with an attractive looking 2.5 mile ridge between the two. Climbing them both in a day, however, would make for a trying adventure. I wish I could supply you with a description of the ridge, but I have no information or experience on what the ridge has to offer. The two peaks are divided by a town quad this one being Raquette Lake and the other being Blue Mountain Lake.

*Via the "Dishrag Pond Trail"
*Trail/Bushwhack
*Blue route

To find the start of the bushwhack you will need to drive down the Cedar River Road for 9 miles to an easement access road. This road is very hard to find, and is not marked, it's more of an old woods road. It was supplied as a route to state land which is just over the hill. I have marked the area on the map provided in this guide. The exact mark for the beginning may not exact, be sure to look closely as you drive through the area, or better yet, scope it out on a different day to save daylight for this climb. Starting from Cedar River Road we immediately started a steep climb up the shoulder of Metcalf Mountain. The road is overgrown with tall grass and ferns making it very hard to see where you're stepping. After about 0.5 miles up this road, we met up with a very well cut property line with state land, we were now clear to go wherever we wished. There is a rumor that there is a public access road from Cedar River Road to state land nearby, we failed to find any such access road. For all we know, we could have been on it.

We followed this property line for only about 50 feet to a trail on the right that looked to be a continuation of an easement road. After that was a very muddy section before we were on a decent footpath. We then followed this footpath for a good distance until we were past the swamp that appeared on our right. This swamp has a very thick shoreline to the SW, so be prepared to have to push yourself through some evergreens and second growth forest. Once past the swamp the woods were very scratchy and thick in places. The forest is very dead below the canopy, and the ground cover is a thick layer of moss. This section went by rather quickly, crossing Brown's Brook along the way.

On the other side of Brown's Brook is another section of scratchy dead woods, which only lasts a few minutes before we immerged into an open hardwood forest. From here it's only a blink to the "Dishrag Pond Trail". The "Dishrag Pond Trail" is nothing more than an old woods road, long retired, but is it a wonderful thing to be on after a battle with the lower elements. Once on this trail we were just E of a gorgeous outlet to an unnamed long pond pictured on the map. The trail meanders away from and back to the marsh pond before climbing a small shoulder.

The "Dishrag Pond Trail" is simply a name informally given to this tract, but doesn't actually go to Dishrag Pond. The trail ends just SE of the pond. Just about 0.1 miles before its end there is an old car in its final resting place just off the trail. From the old car the trail becomes very faint and disappears very quickly in a small section of dead fall.

This is where your navigation skills will be needed. We headed W and crossed the outlet of Dishrag Pond which can be a little tricky depending on the exact point you hit it. We were happy to have come upon a very convenient spot, but looking up and down stream there doesn't seem to be many better places to cross. The water wasn't terribly deep for the most part, so wading could always be an option. From the crossing, the woods seemed a little scratchy again but cleared out nicely to open hardwoods. In fact we moved along very quickly with little or no resistance from the woods. That is until we reached the E facing steep slopes that guarded the summit.

Actually this was a very fun section of the hike. After a little debating we decided to climb right up the slope and emerge upon the S ridge that will guide us right to the summit. Our debating was whether or not we would come upon cliffs that we couldn't overcome along these steep contour lines we saw on the map. We took a shot in the dark and it paid off. We had nothing but solid footing through open hardwoods right to the S ridge. I admit we were sucking wind about every 75-100 vertical feet we climbed but what a sweet spot we were in. The ridge was just as much a joy as the lower sections, a nice open evergreen forest. We just followed along the top of the steep slopes that were on our right and in a heart beat we were standing on the wooded summit of Blue Ridge #99. A small pink ribbon marked the summit for us, placed there by some hiking group of the past. Note; this ribbon may or may not be there in the future. The summit is a little disappointing with no views but the aura is very pleasant. Views can be captured along the descent, which are much easier to see when your back isn't to them.

In route to Blue Ridge #99

The Other 54

Approx. distance from Cedar River Road: 4 miles
Approx. time: 8 to 10 hours RT

Old black spruce forest along the ridge

#100
Brown Pond Mountain
Elevation 3425'
Map #44

I liked Brown Pond Mountain. The route, the pond, the woods, and the summit are all very pleasant and quiet. Brown Pond itself is one of the nicest hidden ponds I've been to in the Adirondacks. This is a great day hike by itself and more of a long stroll than a climb.

*Via Wakely Dam
*Trail/Bushwhack
*Red Route

At Wakely Dam, drive your vehicle across the dam to a small area for parking before a gate. This is now a snowmobile trail and very easy walking. This trail lasts for quite some time; we were on it for 1.7 miles. We left the road in an old clearing. There were branches laid out across the way as if to tell hikers to turn here. There was also an old sign on a tree that was so faint we couldn't read it. Either of these marking could be removed at any time, so please don't depend on them as a point of reference. This spot was at a small crest in the road, prior to it descending back into the woods.

To your left now are the makings of a really old overgrown road, follow it very carefully. There are many old, deep, tire tracks that are filled with water, some knee deep. Most were very hard to see with the deep grass. This road has a few intersections in it, but stay on the more prominent one. After a short distance the road will clean itself up, the grass will be shorter, and the road will almost look used in spots. At 2.1 miles you will see a swamp to your right. Continuing on will bring you to an old field where a farm or camp used to be. Be sure to look around,

243

you can find bits and pieces of history. Now the bushwhack begins.

Jump into the woods and cross the brook to start on your way to Brown Pond. You will now be on a steady climb through open forest, a mix of hardwoods and evergreens. The closer you get to the pond the swampy dead forest appears. You will want to cross the outlet before you approach the shore of the pond; it's much less of a jump if you do. We found a nice rock slab to walk out onto. Once across the outlet you really do need to see Brown Pond; it's quite a nice sight. After taking a few pictures start your climb up the slopes of Brown Pond Mountain. The going is pretty decent, mostly black spruce forest with small fields of ferns to "fernwhack" through. In fact we encountered a few football field sized fern patches. These are gifts when you've been out bushwhacking for a while. The summit approach is a little scratchy but only in a couple small spots, which can be avoided if you look ahead far enough.

Brown Pond

Brown Pond Mountain's summit is fully wooded, as are most of the peaks in the Adirondack 100 Highest in the Indian Lake vicinity. But again it's a very peaceful and relaxing spot for a nice lunch. If you decide to return via the same route beware of a misleading trail. This trail can be found leading from the shore of Brown Pond. It goes directly S and follows close to the shores of the Brown Pond Outlet. This will lead you down to Buell Brook and a hunting camp. Not only that, it's very much out of your way, and a long hike back to your car. Don't make the same mistake we did, there are a ton of old trails in there and this maze will get you walking in circles for hours.

Approx. distance from Wakely Dam: 4 miles
Approx. time: 3.5 to 4 hours, one way
Approx. distance for hike through with Panther and Buell to Rte. 30: 12.5 miles
Approx. time: 10 to 12 hours

*Via Hunting Camp Road
*Road/Bushwhack
*Blue Route
For route description please see Panther via Brown Pond Mountain in the Panther Mountain chapter of this guide (page 70).

The Controversial Two

These two peaks are not part of the official Adirondack 100 Highest list, but at some time may be added to the list, making it 102. At this time they are being used as substitutes for Dun Brook Mountain which is off limits to hikers. Climb these two peaks in place of Dun Brook Mountain.

It is my understanding that Wilmington Peak and Bullhead Mountain are both eligible for the list. But, awaiting further information the list remains unchanged from the 1950's. If the new surveys were used Sawtooth #4 and Brown Pond Mountain would be knocked from the list.

The guidelines to make the list of "The Other 54" is each peak must be at least 0.75 miles from another 100 Highest peak-AND-have a 300' rise on all sides .

So in short, we decided to climb these two peaks to see what they were all about. Not because they are part of the Adirondack 100 Highest but because they are there.

#101
Wilmington Peak
Elevation 3458'
Map #42

Wilmington Peak may someday replace Sawtooth #4. I personally feel Sawtooth #4 is much nicer and worthy than this one. But access for Wilmington Peak is much easier, making it an easy half days outing to get this one along with Morgan. The route for Wilmington Peak starts from Cooper Kill Pond in Wilmington. This peak is right in the heart of the Stevenson Range in the shadows of Whiteface Mountain. To access the trailhead, see the chapter on Morgan Mountain (page 237).

*Via Cooper Kill Pond Trail
*Trail/Bushwhack
*Green Route

As with Morgan Mountain, the trail starts off along an old jeep/4-wheeler trail and is quite flat with very little elevation change for the first 0.5 miles. The trail starts to climb moderately through the Stevenson Range and becomes much rockier and steeper as the height of land is approached at 1.85 miles. From the height of land the trail descends very moderately to the shore of Cooper Kill Pond. From this side you will need to cross a small stream and a wet beaver area, along the base of a dam to reach the lean-to.

From here, continue to hike along the trail for approximately another 100' past the lean-to. All while watching for a small herd path. This herd path will take you around the pond to a few view points. Once you are around the the pond you should be able to see the herd path clearly. Start heading just E of N along the long ridge of Wilmington Peak. You will start climbing quite seriously above the pond for about 100' before

247

it levels off in an open woods forest. At this point you will want to keep yourself to the E side of the ridge and look for an obvious herd path. This herd path will get you through the blowdown along the ridge and deliver you all the way to the summit.

Wilmington Peak behind Cooper Kill Pond

The odd thing is why is there a obvious and well used herd path to an unnamed summit, which is totally wooded and has mediocre views. It's not a game trail it's too continually obvious. Maybe campers at the lean-to or other fools like us?? If anyone has the answer please let me know.

Catamount Mountain from the Wilmington Peak Ridge

The Other 54

Anyhow, along the ridge there is a wonderful view of Catamount. If you've never seen Catamount or been there you're missing a great little hike. From the other side there is a decent view of Whiteface and Esther with Morgan in the foreground. The ridge, as I said, has a nice herd path along its entirety, but otherwise the woods were very open-minus two small blowdown sections that could have been easily circumnavigated. Be sure not to mistake the first bump as the summit. Keep going a little further for the actual top.

Approx. Distance from Cooper Kill Pond: 0.7 miles
Approx. Time from Cooper Kill Pond: 1.5 to 2 hours RT

Puffer Mountain from Bullhead Mountain

#102
Bullhead Mountain
Elevation 3432'
Map #45

Bullhead can be found E of Chimney Mountain and N of Puffer Mountain in the Indian Lake region. Bullhead is one long ridge whose highest point is on the southern most peak. With a combination of the two route described below, a wonderful loop can be hiked with a few, small viewpoints to take in. This peak is unofficially #102, but who's counting.

*The Southwest Ridge
*Trail/Bushwhack
*Red Route

It was a very cold, frost bitten day in October, and our breath floating in the air before us. We ventured out to see what Bullhead Mountain was all about. We started from Kings Flow in Indian Lake; which is also the trailhead for Puffer Mountain and Chimney Mountain. The trail to Puffer Pond is at the back right of the parking area.

The trail at first follows a road, for a short distance until coming to a bridge over a small brook. We soon came to a fork in the foot trail; right is the fork we needed to follow. After a small descent we were following a lightly used and wet trail. This trail was slightly under attack by blow down, some large stuff, but mostly a littering of branches.

Then at 0.5 miles we crossed Carroll Brook, a much smaller inlet that the one we crossed at 0.7 miles. This one took a little negotiating. We had to go down stream a bit to find a place to jump across. Thankfully we did, because the brook was rather deep and the water cold as ice. Upstream to the E we could see Bullhead Mountain, our destination for the day.

We continued along the trail through a couple marshy areas, and along Carroll Brook for another 0.3 miles before the trail turned SE. It's was another quick 0.3 miles to the intersection with the John Pond Trail. From here though, is where the climbing begins. From here we had a 200' climb to a col along Bullhead's ridge. Atop the col we rested, and had an energy snack before we tackled the untrailed route to Bullhead. The woods here are very open; hardwoods with a light scattering of small soft evergreens. A light game path led us through any tight spots.

This first 0.6 miles is pretty moderate, not to steep. The footing is very stable, only a light cover of freshly fallen leaves. There were no cliffs to worry about, no real significant amount of blow down or dead fall to fuss with. A very pleasant walk in the park, with no one else around. We did encounter some small lookouts along the E side of the ridge, adding to the pleasant experience. However; the remaining 0.3 miles to the summit got a little tricky. We encountered a few small shelves to climb, and the dead fall seemed to double along this section. Not to mention the woods seemed to change before our eyes. One minute wide open hardwoods, the next, thicker spruce invading our space. But it's all good. After this section the terrain seems to flatten out a bit along the ridge for the remaining 0.15 miles to the summit. But the woods are still a little tight and scratchy. The summit doesn't offer much for views, small ones toward Puffer Mountain and Buck Mountain, and that's only by standing on a lone downed tree.

Approx. distance from trailhead: 2.75 miles
Approx. time: 5 to 6 hours RT

*Via the West Slopes
*Trail/Bushwhack
*Black Route

We used the W slopes to bail off the mountain when conditions were just turning against us on a really cold fall day. We found out this just maybe the ticket to a wonderful climb.

From the summit we took a bearing W, fought the thicker woods of the summit crown, and descended rather steeply toward the John Pond Trail. The forest opened up rather nicely into hardwoods. The ground was covered in dry leaves; we must have sounded like a herd of elephants coming down off the mountain.

At roughly 0.45 miles from the summit we crossed over a very dry inlet of Carroll Brook. At about this time the lay of the land started to ease. The terrain isn't quite as steep, and there are many saplings growing amongst the older trees. Then at 0.65 miles we were on relatively flat land.

We started looking for the trail early so we wouldn't cross over it. Well, it was a good idea. We still managed to cross over the trail. John Pond Trail is used very lightly, and is difficult to see in the fall with leaves covering the track. From John Pond Trail we followed it S about 0.25 miles to the Puffer Pond Trail, and from there back to our car along the same route we came in.

To use this route as an ascent route, follow the distances and descriptions in reverse.

Approx. distance from trailhead: 2.6 miles
Approx. time 5 to 5.5 hours RT
Approx. distance for loop with SW Ridge Route: 5.25 miles
Approx, time for loop: 5 to 5.5 hours

View from the summit of Bullhead Mountain

The Other 54 Checklist

#	Mountain	Ht.	USGS Quad	Date
47	MacNaughton	4000'	Ampersand Lake	
48	Green	3980'	Elizabethtown	
49	Lost Pond	3900'	Ampersand Lake	
50	Moose	3899'	Saranac Lake	
51	Snowy	3899'	Indian Lake	
52	Kilburn	3892'	Lake Placid	
53	Sawtooth #1	3877'	Ampersand Lake	
54	Panther	3865'	Indian Lake	
55	McKenzie	3861'	Saranac Lake	
56	Blue Ridge	3860'	Indian Lake	
57	North River	3860'	Mount Marcy	
58	Sentinel	3838'	Lake Placid	
59	Lyon	3830'	Moffitsville	
60	Sawtooth #2	3820'	Ampersand Lake	
61	TR	3820'	Mount Marcy	
62	Averill	3810'	Lyon Mountain	
63	Avalanche	3800'	Mount Marcy	
64	Buell	3786'	Indian Lake	
65	Boreas	3776'	Mount Marcy	
66	Blue	3760'	Blue Mtn. Lake	
67	Wakely	3760'	Wakely Mountain	
68	Henderson	3752'	Santanoni Peak	
69	Lewey	3742'	Indian Lake	
70	Sawtooth #3	3700'	Ampersand Lake	
71	Wallface	3700'	Ampersand Lake	
72	Hurricane	3694'	Elizabethtown	
73	Hoffman	3693'	Blue Ridge	
74	Cheny Cobble	3683'	Mount Marcy	
75	Calamity	3620'	Santanoni Peak	
76	Little Moose	3620'	Wakley Mountain	

#	Mountain	Ht.	USGS Quad	Date
77	Sunrise	3614'	Mount Marcy	
78	Stewart	3602'	Lake Placid	
79	Jay	3600'	Lewis	
80	Pitchoff	3600'	Keene Valley	
81	Saddleback	3600'	Lewis	
82	Pillsbury	3597'	W. Canada Lakes	
83	Slide	3584'	Lake Placid	
84	Gore	3583'	Thirteemth Lake	
85	Dun Brook	3580'	Deerland	
86	Noonmark	3556'	Santanoni Peak	
87	Adams	3540'	Blue Mtn. Lake	
88	Fishing Brook #1	3540'	Deerland	
89	Little Santanoni	3500'	Santanoni Peak	
90	Blue Ridge	3497'	Blue Mtn. Lake	
91	Fishing Brook #2	3480'	Deerland	
92	Puffer	3472'	Thirteenth Lake	
93	Sawtooth #4	3460'	Ampersand Lake	
94	Sawtooth #5	3460'	Ampersand Lake	
95	Wolf Pond	3460'	Blue Ridge	
96	Cellar	3447'	Wakely Mountain	
97	Blue Ridge	3440'	Blue Ridge	
98	Morgan	3440'	Wilmington	
99	Blue Ridge	3436'	Raquette Lake	
100	Brown Pond	3425'	Indian Lake	
101	Wilmington	3458'	Wilmington	
102	Bullhead	3432'	Thirteenth Lake	

View from Slide Mountain

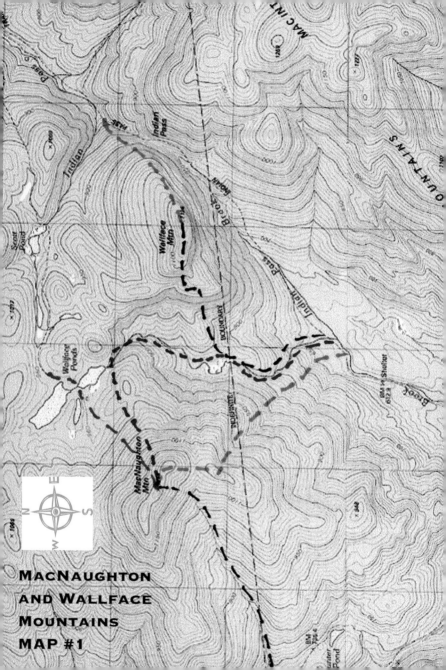

**MacNaughton
and Wallface
Mountains
Map #1**

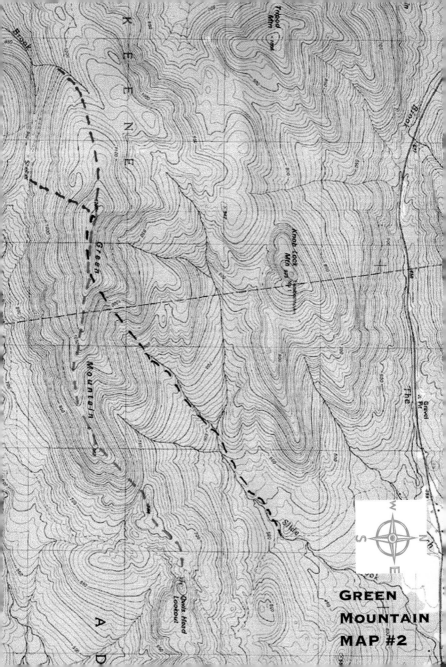

GREEN
MOUNTAIN
MAP #2

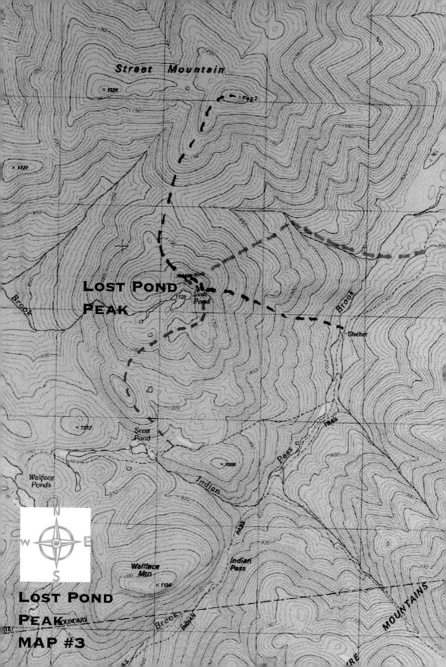

Street Mountain

LOST POND
PEAK

Lost Pond

Brook

Brook

Shelter

Scott
Pond

Indian

Wallface
Ponds

Pass

Wallface
Mtn

Indian
Pass

MOUNTAINS

Brook

Indian

BOUNDARY

LOST POND
PEAK
MAP #3

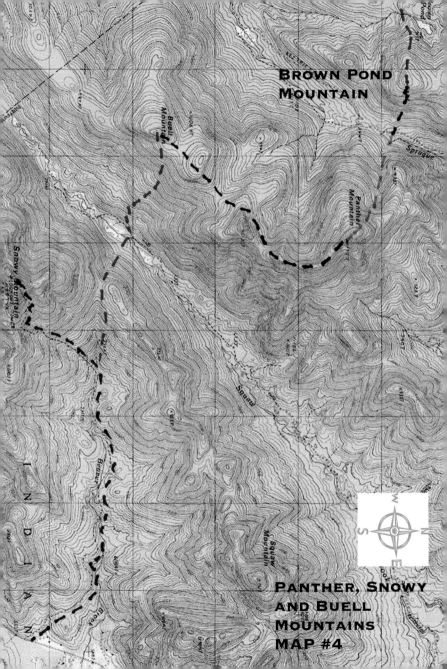

BROWN POND
MOUNTAIN

PANTHER, SNOWY
AND BUELL
MOUNTAINS
MAP #4

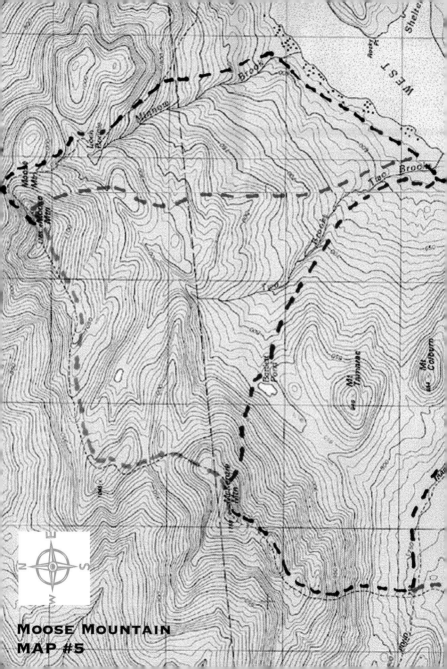

MOOSE MOUNTAIN
MAP #5

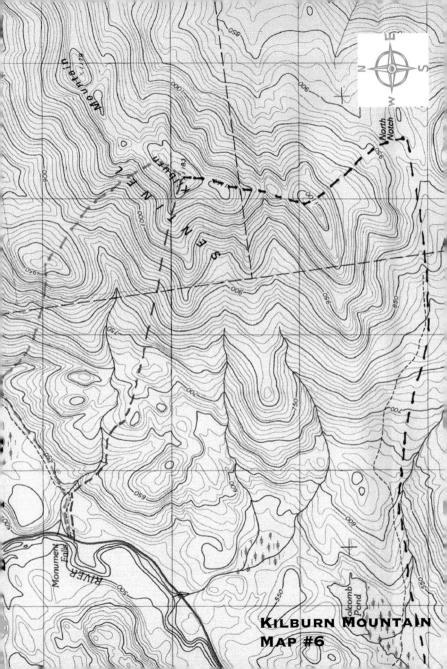

KILBURN MOUNTAIN
MAP #6

Alford Mtn

SAWTOOTH #1

SAWTOOTH #1
MAP #7

MOUNTAINS

PAR

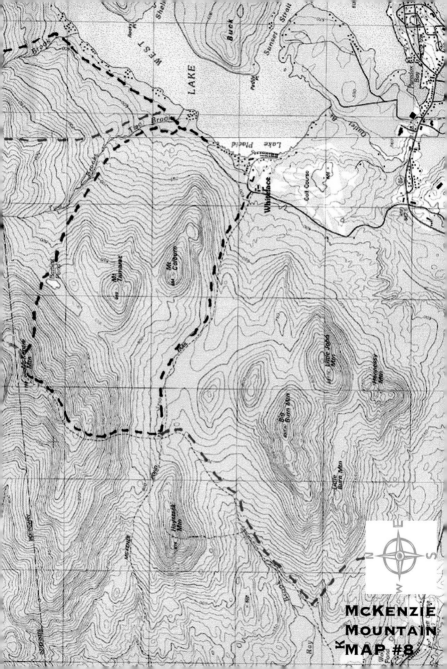

McKenzie
Mountain
MAP #8

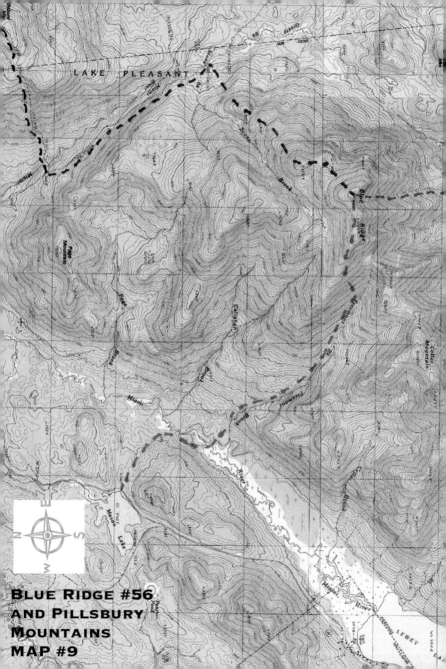

LAKE PLEASANT

BLUE RIDGE #56
AND PILLSBURY
MOUNTAINS
MAP #9

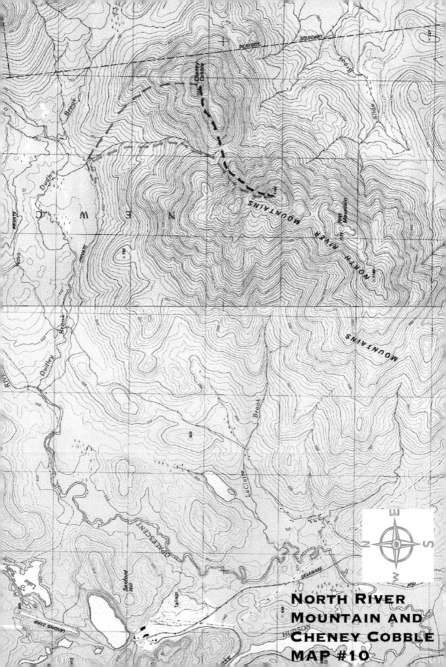

NORTH RIVER
MOUNTAIN AND
CHENEY COBBLE
MAP #10

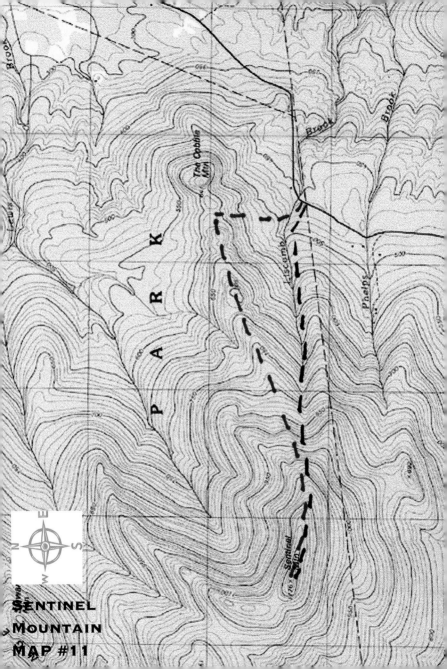

SENTINEL
MOUNTAIN
MAP #11

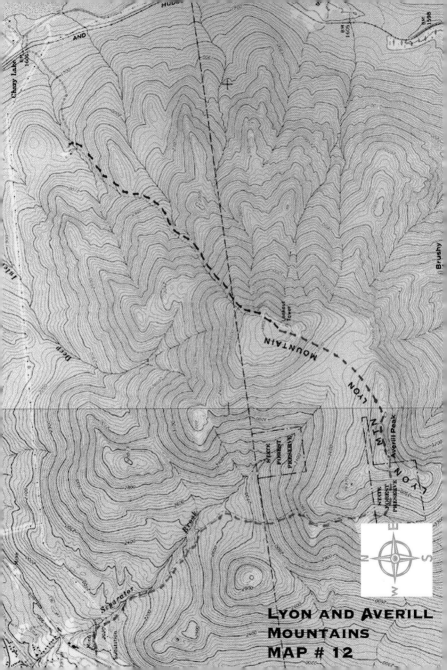

LYON AND AVERILL
MOUNTAINS
MAP # 12

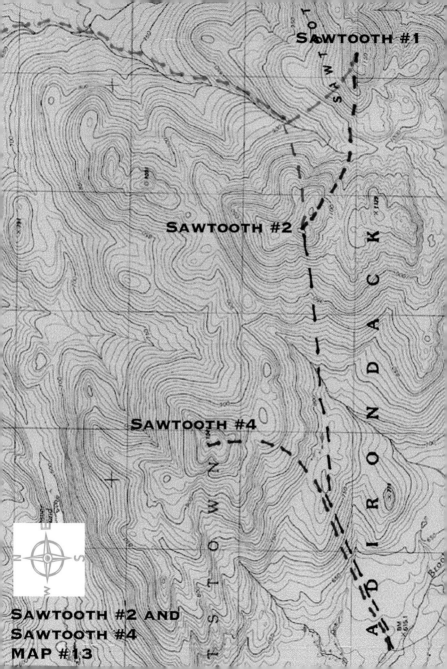

SAWTOOTH #1

SAWTOOTH #2

SAWTOOTH #4

SAWTOOTH #2 AND
SAWTOOTH #4
MAP #13

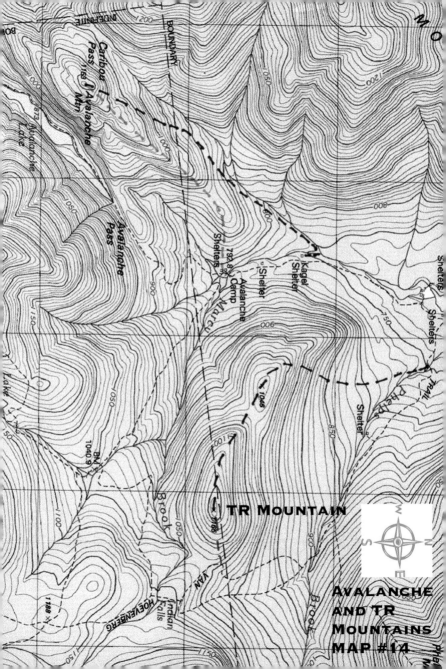

BOREAS MOUNTAIN

BOREAS MOUNTAIN

BOREAS
MOUNTAIN
MAP #15

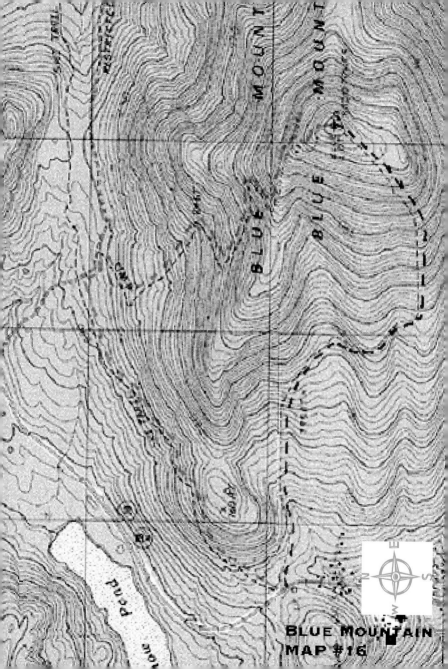

BLUE MOUNTAIN
MAP #16

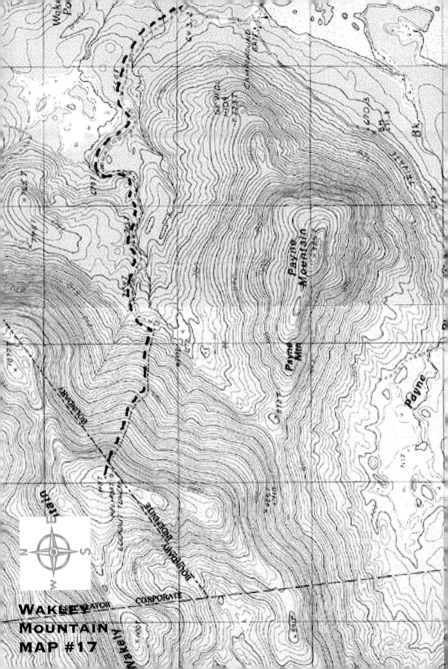

WAKELY
MOUNTAIN
MAP #17

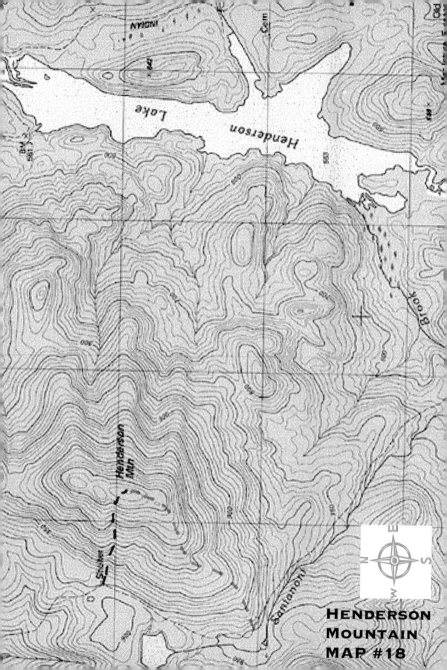

INDIAN

Cem

BM

Henderson Lake

Brook

Henderson Mtn

Santanoni

Student

HENDERSON MOUNTAIN MAP #18

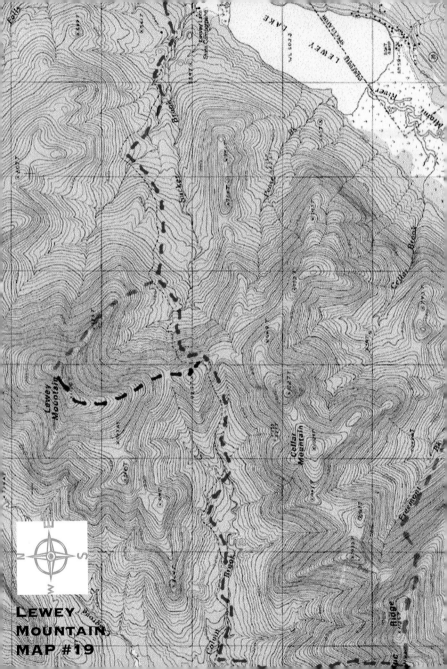

LEWEY
MOUNTAIN
MAP #19

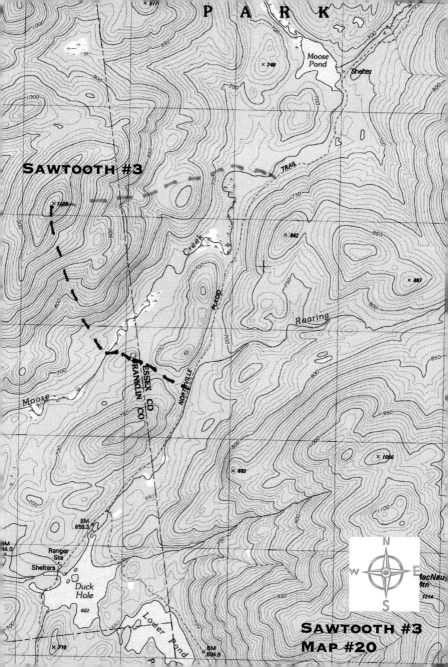

P A R K

Moose
Pond

Shelter

× 749

Sawtooth #3

TRAIL

× 1189

× 842

750

850

Creek

× 887

Roaring

ESSEX CO
FRANKLIN CO

NORTHVILLE PLACID

Moose

× 883

× 1086

950

1100

BM
659.3

Ranger
Sta

Shelters

Duck
Hole

662

× 710

Lower Pond

BM
884.9

N
W E
S

MacNau
Mtn
1214

Sawtooth #3
Map #20

CROW
CLEARING

Shelter

Lost
Pond

× 927

Brook

INDEFINITE   BOUNDARY

× 1014

ELIZABETHTOWN

952

Chase
Mtn   971

Conners
Notch

1061

950

Shelter

Shelter

Hurricane
Mtn
Lookout
Tower
1121

× 852

× 844

Pitchoff
Mtn

845 ×

× 696

N
W   E
S

Gravel
Pit

HURRICANE
MOUNTAIN
MAP #21

458

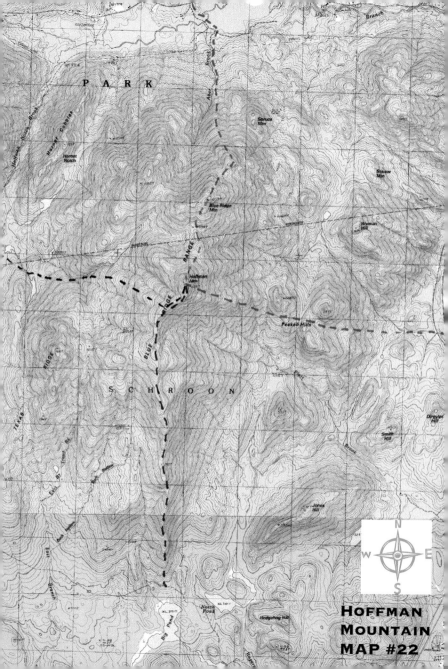

PARK

Spruce
Mtn

Shaw
Mtn

Blue Ridge
Mtn

Wyman
Hill

RANGE

Hoffman
Mtn

BLUE RIDGE

Peaked Hills

SCHROON

Dingley
Hill

Smith
Hill

**HOFFMAN
MOUNTAIN
MAP #22**

Open Hardwood Forest

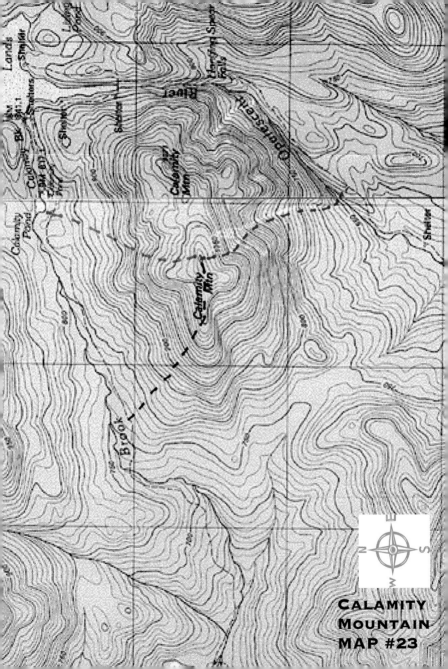

CALAMITY
MOUNTAIN
MAP #23

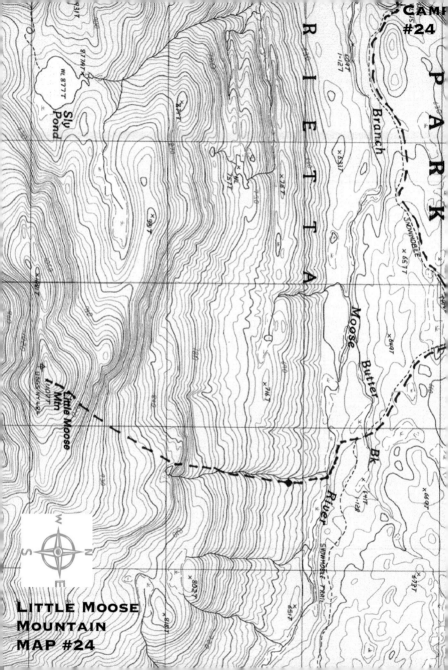

MARIETTA

PARK

Branch

SNOWMOBILE

Moose

Butter

Bk

Moose River

SNOWMOBILE TRAIL

Sly
Pond

Little Moose
Mtn

LITTLE MOOSE
MOUNTAIN
MAP #24

SUNRISE
MOUNTAIN
MAP #25

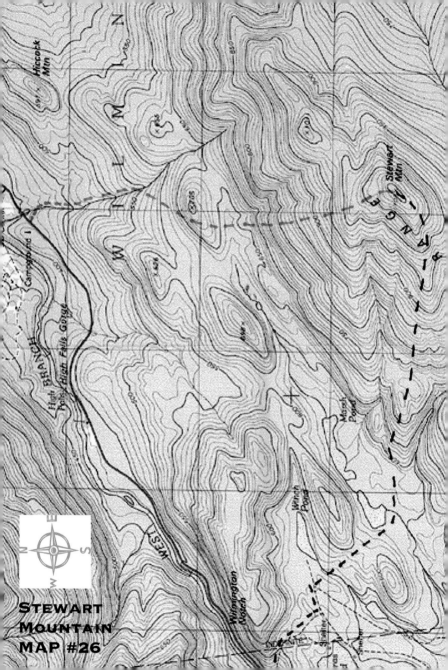

Hiccok Mtn

WILM

Campground

High Falls Gorge

Douglas

BRANCH

WEST

Wilmington Notch

RANGE

Stewart Mtn

Marsh Pond

Winch Pond

N
E
W
S

**STEWART
MOUNTAIN
MAP #26**

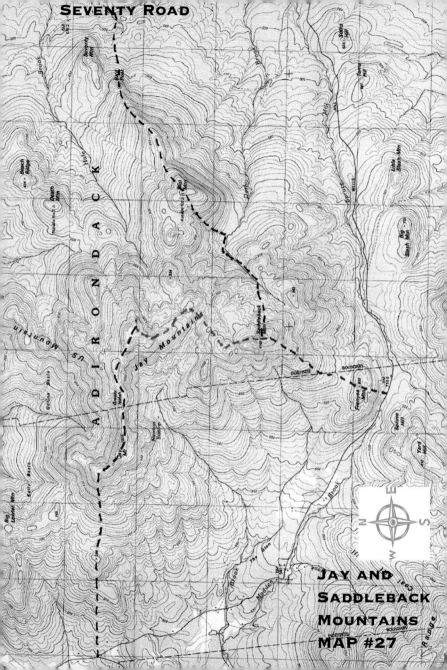

SEVENTY ROAD

JAY AND
SADDLEBACK
MOUNTAINS
MAP #27

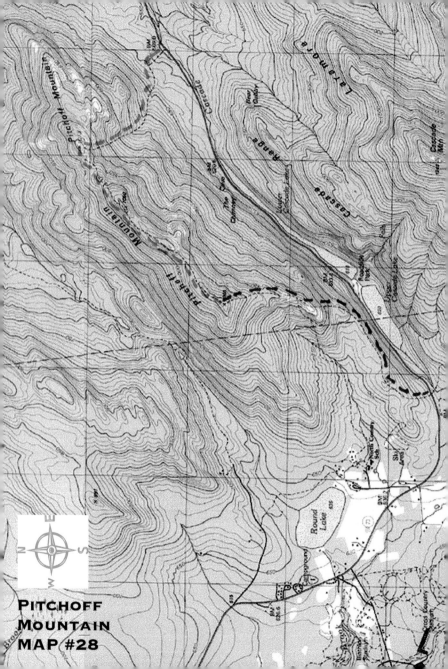

PITCHOFF
MOUNTAIN
MAP #28

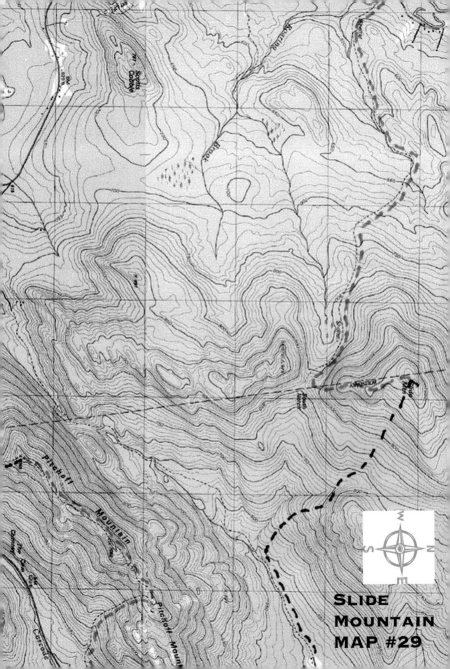

SLIDE
MOUNTAIN
MAP #29

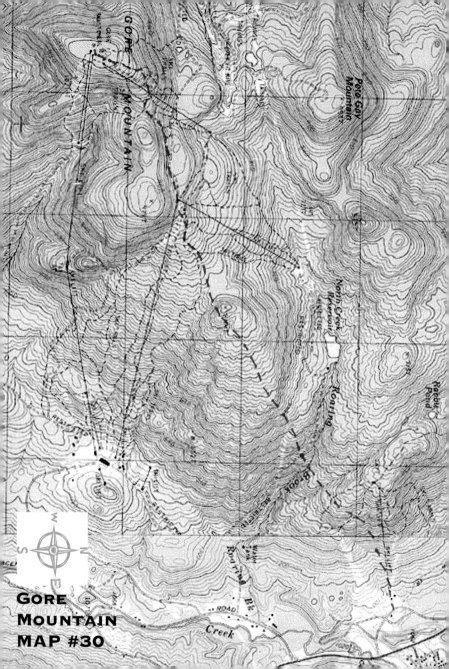

GORE
MOUNTAIN
MAP #30

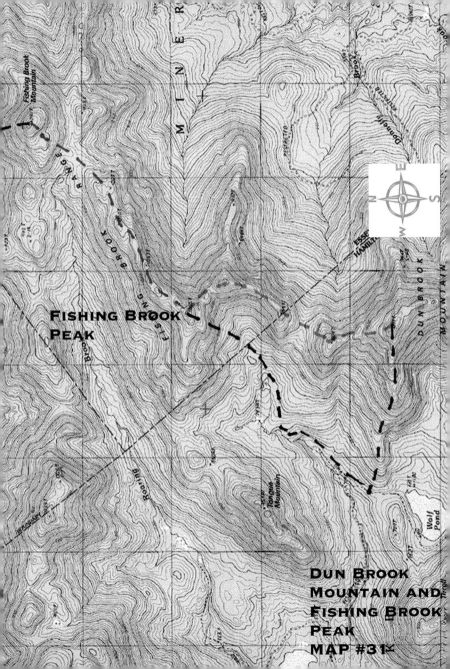

FISHING BROOK
PEAK

DUN BROOK
MOUNTAIN AND
FISHING BROOK
PEAK
MAP #31

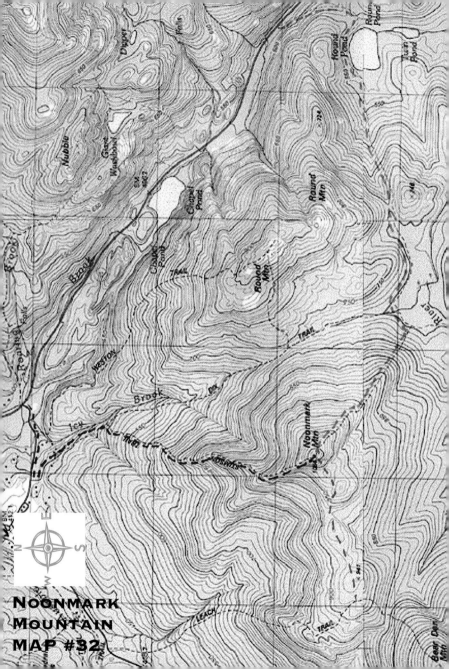

NOONMARK
MOUNTAIN
MAP #32

Popple Hill

Mount Adams

Lookout Tower

RIVER

Lake Jimmy

Lake Sally

STRIP

Cem

Old Mine Imper Furnace

RIVER

MOUNT
ADAMS
MAP #33

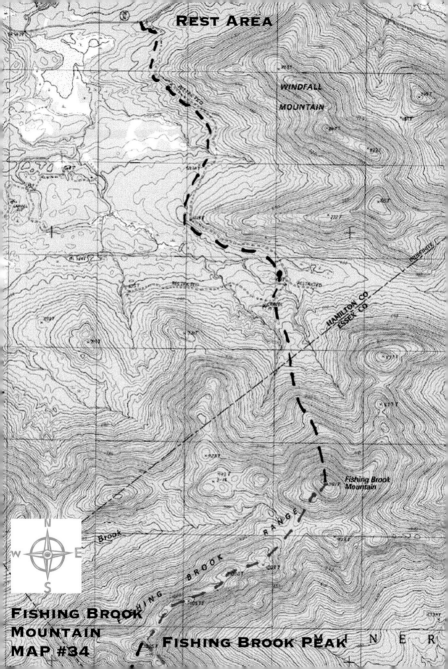

REST AREA

WINDFALL
MOUNTAIN

HAMILTON CO
ESSEX CO

Fishing Brook
Mountain

RANGE

Brook

FISHING BROOK

FISHING BROOK
MOUNTAIN
MAP #34

FISHING BROOK PEAK

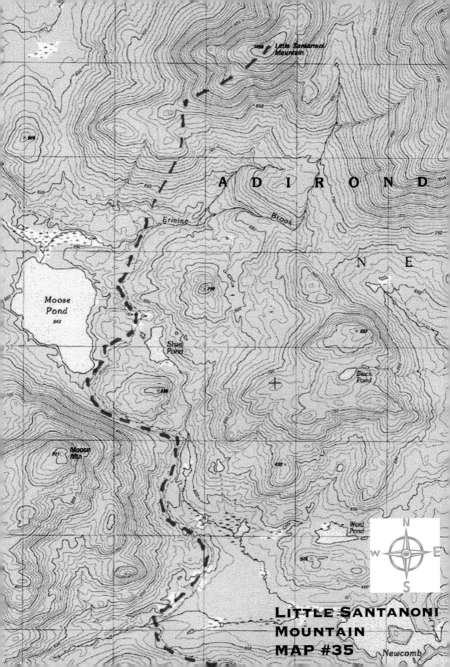

A D I R O N D

N E

Little Santanoni
Mountain

Moose Pond

Shan Pond

Black Pond

Ermine

Brook

Moose Mtn

Ward Pond

Newcomb

LITTLE SANTANONI
MOUNTAIN
MAP #35

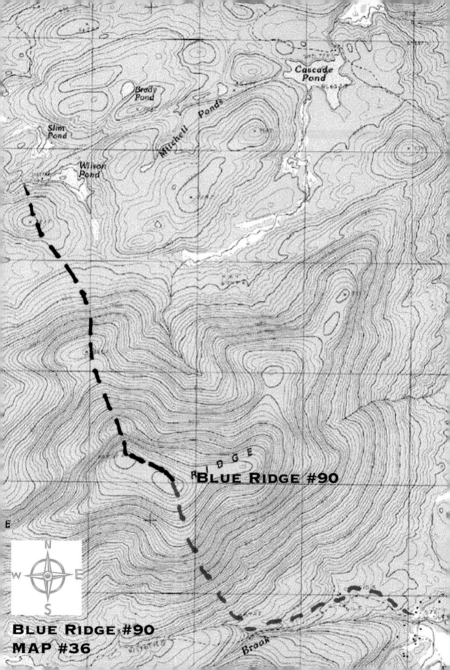

Cascade
Pond

Brady
Pond

Slim
Pond

Mitchell Ponds

Wilson
Pond

R I D G E

BLUE RIDGE #90

N
W E
S

BLUE RIDGE #90
MAP #36

Brook

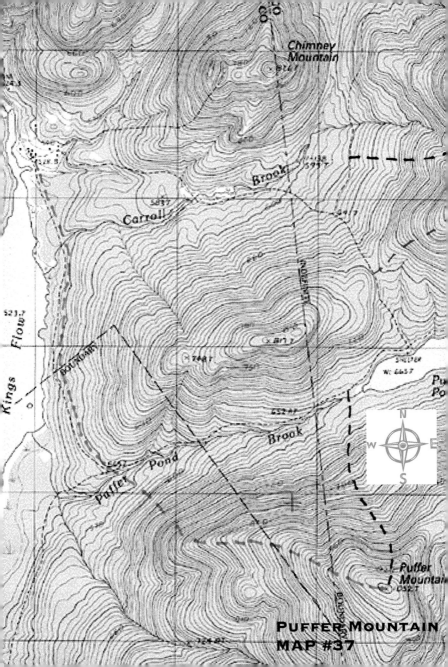

Chimney
Mountain

Brook

Carroll

Kings Flow

BOUNDARY

Puffer
Pond

Brook

Pu
Po

Puffer
Mountain

PUFFER MOUNTAIN
MAP #37

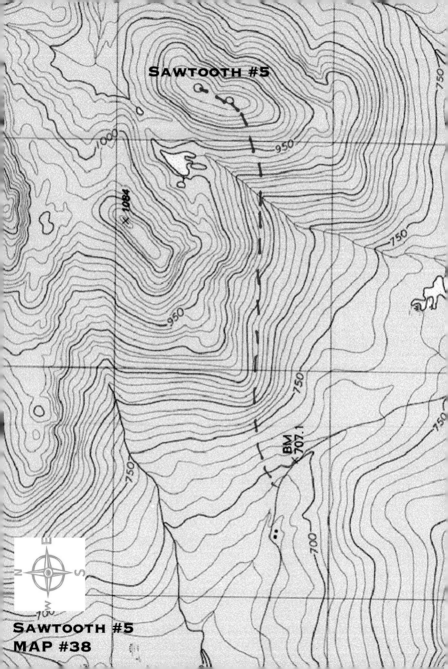

Sawtooth #5

Sawtooth #5
MAP #38

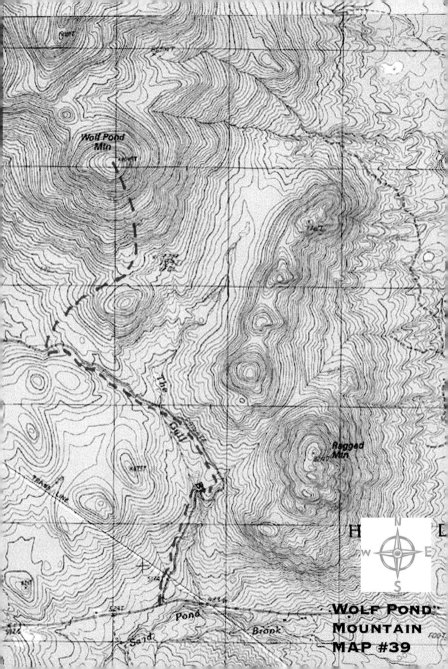

Wolf Pond Mtn

The Z

Ragged Mtn

The Gulf

TRANS LINE

Pond

Brook

Sard.

N
W E
S

**WOLF POND
MOUNTAIN
MAP #39**

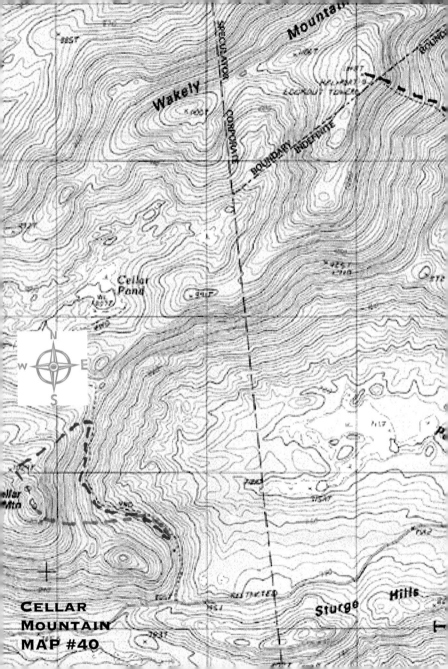

Wakely Mountain

SPECULATOR

CORPORATE

BOUNDARY

BOUNDARY

LOOKOUT TOWER

Cellar Pond

Cellar Mtn

RESTRICTED

Sturge Hills

CELLAR MOUNTAIN MAP #40

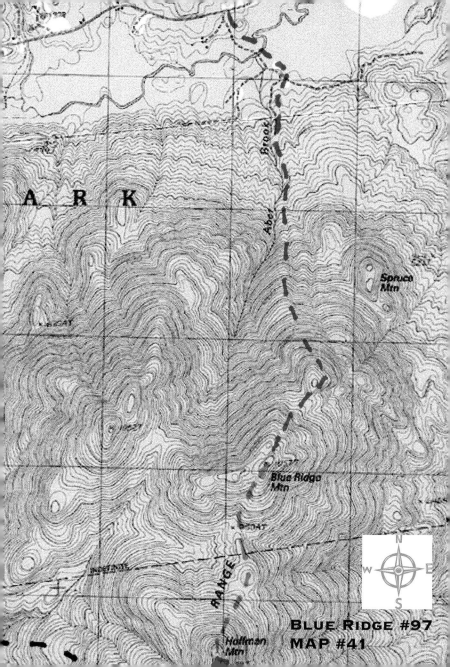

A R K

Brook

Abes

Spruce
Mtn

KILLCAT

Blue Ridge
Mtn

RANGE

WOLFHILL

N
W   E
S

BLUE RIDGE #97
MAP #41

Hoffman
Mtn

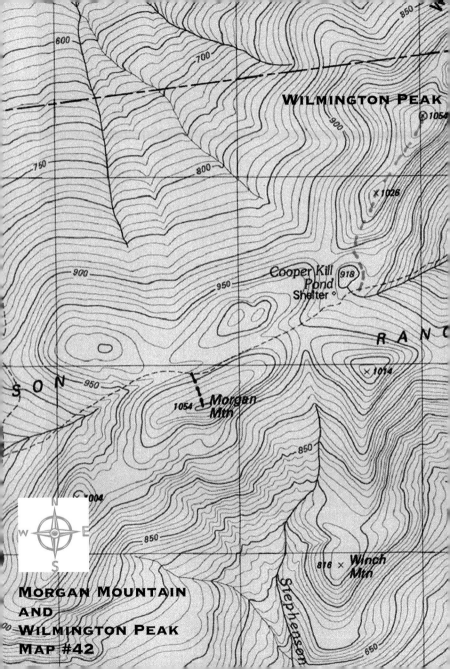

WILMINGTON PEAK

⊗ 1054

× 1026

Cooper Kill
Pond
Shelter ○   918

R A N ○

× 1014

S O N

1054 ∙ Morgan
         Mtn

850

∙ 004

850

816 × Winch
          Mtn

Stephensen

650

N
W   E
S

MORGAN MOUNTAIN
AND
WILMINGTON PEAK
MAP #42

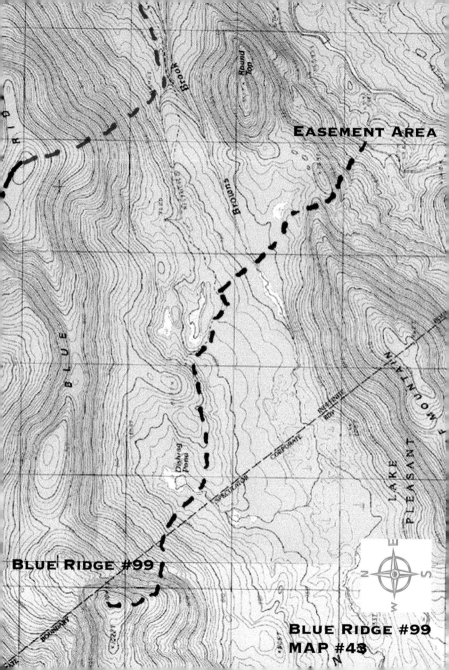

EASEMENT AREA

Round Top

BLUE RIDGE #99

BLUE RIDGE #99
MAP #43

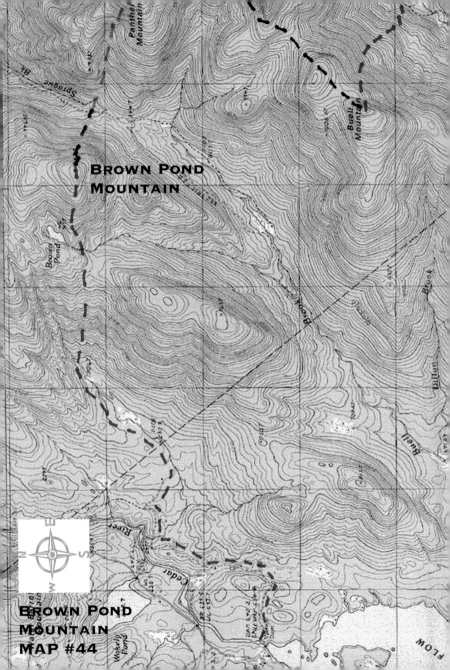

BROWN POND
MOUNTAIN

Panther Mountain

Sprague Bk.

Buell Mountain

Brown Pond

Brook

Dillon Brook

Buell Mountain

River

Cedar

Wakely Pond

N
E
S
W

BROWN POND
MOUNTAIN
MAP #44